# Manchester United

## BUILDING A LEGEND: THE BUSBY YEARS

# Manchester United

## BUILDING A LEGEND: THE BUSBY YEARS

EDWARD ENSOR
RESEARCH BY ALAN PINNOCK

PHOTOGRAPHS BY THE
**Daily Mail**

ATLANTIC WORLD

Published by Atlantic World in 2014

Atlantic Publishing
38 Copthorne Road, Croxley Green
Hertfordshire, WD3 4AQ, UK

© Atlantic Publishing
All images © Associated Newspapers Archive
except pages: 12(b), 50(t), 51(t&b), 84(b), 120(t&b) and
front cover © Getty Images

A catalogue record for this book is available
from the British Library.

Hardback back ISBN 978-1-909242-32-6
Paperback ISBN 978-1-909242-12-8

Printed in China

# Contents

# Setting the stage for the Theatre of Dreams

**M**anchester United fans could have been forgiven for viewing the February 1945 appointment of Alexander Matthew Busby with a sceptical eye. If this was the new managerial broom that would sweep United back to the top after a generation among the also-rans, Reds' fans had heard it before. And they had heard it from incoming bosses who, unlike Busby, could boast a track record in running a club. Why should the 35-year-old former Manchester City and Liverpool star succeed when so many others had failed, especially as he was inheriting a mountain of debt, a bombed-out stadium and a team best known for yo-yoing between Divisions One and Two in the interwar years?

It proved to be an inspired decision on the part of the board. Busby was in the vanguard of a new breed of manager, out on the training ground in his tracksuit at a time when many a boss's kit included a buttonhole and spats. More importantly, he had a vision of how the game should be played, with the emphasis on skill and pace. 'Nobody stops the ball except the goalkeeper' was a favourite maxim. Ball-playing forwards were converted into defenders to ensure that flair ran throughout the side. There were no chalk boards with complex diagrams or elaborate team talks. Busby gave his gifted players licence to express themselves, never losing sight of the fact that football was part of the entertainment business. It was a philosophy that attracted hordes of new fans, including the teenage Duncan Edwards, who eschewed his local side, Wolves, in order to become part of the swashbuckling Old Trafford set.

The pioneering adventures in the fledgling European Cup confirmed the 'Busby Babes' as the glamour side of English football, while the Munich disaster played its part in giving United a unique standing among the footballing fraternity.

Busby built three magnificent, championship-winning sides during his 25-year reign, and did it on a shoestring. The team that won the 1948 FA Cup was assembled for less than £8,000, while the 'Babes' who lined up at Wembley nine years later cost a mere £50,000. It is sometimes said that the marvellous sixties' side was a chequebook team, yet eight of the eleven who were instantly immortalized with the 4-1 victory over Benfica in 1968 were home grown. The entire European Cup-winning team cost less than Spurs paid Southampton for Martin Chivers that same season.

Busby recognized that his legacy would endure. 'United is no longer just a football club,' he said, when he stepped down in 1969, 'it is an institution.' Unquestionably, he created an aura which pervades the club to this day. It was Bobby Charlton who described Old Trafford as the 'Theatre of Dreams', but it was Matt Busby who set the stage.

# Beginnings:
# 1878–1945

'HE WILL BUILD up the team and put it right where it belongs – at the top.' Such was the bold claim of Manchester United secretary Walter Crickmer after watching Company Sergeant-Major Matthew Busby sign on the dotted line on 19 February 1945 and agree to become the club's eighth manager. Of course, there is no great track record of football club officials welcoming a managerial appointment with expectations of ineptitude and dross. To what extent Crickmer truly believed the 35-year-old rookie manager would meet the challenge of his rallying cry is a matter of conjecture, though by the time the long-serving secretary lost his life at Munich 13 years later, Busby had already comfortably exceeded the goal mapped out on that winter's day as the century's second global conflict was drawing to a close. Crickmer never lived to see the stellar achievements of the 1960s side, which not only put United

'where it belongs' in terms of the domestic game, but on top of the European pile, too. Busby had delivered in triplicate, but more than that, he never lost sight of the fact that he was in an entertainment as well as a results business. He created the yardstick against which all United sides since have been measured. The team might not always be victorious, but it can always play the game the United way.

The ethos of the club was hardly at the forefront of anyone's mind when it came into existence in 1878. The railwaymen who turned out for Newton Heath Lancashire and Yorkshire Cricket and Football Club took to the field after a day's toil, as did any number of factory workers with a love of the round-ball game in that era. The 'Heathens' became a professional outfit in 1885 but didn't make the invitational cut when League football kicked off three years later. In 1889 the club joined the game's second tier, the Football Alliance, while continuing to knock on the door to gain admittance to the top table. After several failed applications, Newton Heath took their place among the country's elite in 1892. The Football League adopted the Alliance wholesale as its new Second Division, and the Heathens were awarded one of the two places up for grabs as the First was expanded to 16 teams.

### VICTORY AND DEFEAT IN 'TEST MATCH'

It was a baptism of fire as the club found itself marooned at the foot of the table in each of its first two seasons. Newton Heath preserved their top-flight status in 1892-3 by beating Second Division champions Small Heath in the play-offs, but a year later swapped places with Liverpool, who defeated them in the same 'Test Match' arena. First blood to the men from up the East Lancs Road.

The club began distancing itself from its roots with a move away from its mudbath ground in North Road, Newton Heath, at the end of its inaugural season in the Football League. The new facility, across the city in Bank Street, Clayton, was barely more adequate, another desperately poor pitch that was regularly engulfed in the noxious fumes that issued from adjacent smokestacks. Despite its shortcomings as a premier-class sporting venue, Clayton remained home to the club for the next sixteen years. This period encompassed the first golden age – in fact, the only sustained period of success that the club enjoyed prior to Busby's arrival. It also witnessed the establishment of a reconstituted club with a new name rising from the ashes of the defunct Newton Heath FC.

After suffering the drop in 1893-94, Newton Heath remained in Division Two for the next eight seasons. They flirted with a return to the top flight on a number of occasions,

Matt Busby had an indifferent start to his career as an inside-forward with Manchester City. He blossomed after converting to wing-half and became one of the greats of the prewar era. His experience stood him in good stead in his managerial career, for he never pigeon-holed players regarding position. Indeed, he made a number of astute positional changes which served the team well and gave players a new lease of life.

and twice missed out after reaching the play-offs. But as the new century dawned the picture was bleak. In 1900-01 the team finished in the bottom half of the table for the first time, and was reduced to holding a four-day mid-season bazaar to address a worsening financial crisis and fund the purchase of new players. No angle was overlooked; club captain Harry Stafford even strapped a collection tin to the neck of his St

Bernard, which wandered round the exhibits in St James's Hall. Instead of raising a few shillings, Stafford's enterprise led to an act of salvation. The dog wandered off and found its way into the possession of the owner of the Manchester Brewery Company, John Henry Davies, who took a shine both to the hound, and, once he had traced its rightful owner, to the club. Davies made a contribution in exchange for being allowed to keep the dog, and gave Stafford assurances of further help. Within a year the Newton Heath captain had need to call in that favour to prevent the club from going to the wall.

### HEATHENS' PRESIDENT CALLS IN RECEIVERS

In 1901-02 the club's form slumped still further and the Heathens finished 15th in an 18-strong division. Nor was the crisis confined to the field. The Manchester weather conspired to dampen the enthusiasm of supporters, who stayed away in droves for attractive fixtures that should have boosted the coffers. The club had racked up over £2500 in debts and in January 1902 a winding-up order was granted at the behest of creditors, whose number included Newton Heath president William Healey. Some club officials - and the Manchester Evening News - thought Healey acted precipitately in trying to recover the £242 17s 10d he was owed. With bankruptcy proceedings hanging over their heads, the directors manfully tried to extricate the club from the mire. Their cause wasn't helped by the Football League, whose response to the litigation proceedings was to close the ground and postpone a home match against Middlesbrough, thus depriving the club of much needed funds. On 18 January 1902 a whip-round was needed to finance an away trip to Bristol City, which resulted in a 4-0 defeat.

Newton Heath managed to keep its head above water until 18 March, when a crisis meeting was called. Harry Stafford got the biggest cheer of the night when he announced the names of five men who would each put £200 into the club. Stafford himself was one, Davies another. It wasn't pure altruism. The benefactors wanted control of the club in return, and the new custodians took over in a relatively seamless transition, with John Henry Davies assuming the position of chairman. Reorganisation raised the thorny issue of renaming the club. It was important for the new solvent regime to distance itself from its indebted predecessor. There was also the problem of visiting teams and fans heading to Newton Heath, only to find they faced a mad dash across town in time for kick-off against their Clayton opposition. Manchester Central and Manchester Celtic were floated and dismissed, as was Manchester FC, which happened to be the name of the local rugby club. Louis Rocca, a registered player who never made it into the first team, then made a suggestion: Manchester United. It met with widespread support, as did the proposal that the newly constituted team should play in red shirts. 43 years later, Rocca would target Busby as the man to take the club forward after the fallow interwar years, and thus holds a special place in the club's roll of honour on two counts.

### MANGNALL TAKES OVER

The first league campaign under the Manchester United banner, 1902-03, saw the team enjoy an immediate improvement in fortunes, finishing fifth. But the great leap forward began with the arrival of Ernest Mangnall from Burnley early the following season. Mangnall was United's first real manager; until then, the club secretary was responsible for team matters. He was of the school that believed in ball

Billy Meredith, 'the Welsh Wizard', is widely regarded as the game's first superstar. He helped United win the FA Cup in 1909 and the championship in 1910-11.

starvation during training, making players hungry when Saturday came. A team should not have 'too many wee men', and star players with inflated opinions of themselves were liabilities that a manager could do without. He imposed a structure that reaped great dividends. After twice narrowly missing out on promotion, United secured a return to the top division in 1905-06. Then, after one season of consolidation, United claimed their first championship, running away with the title by nine points. With 13 wins in the first 14 games, including a 6-1 away victory over reigning champions Newcastle United, the team set a scorching pace that no other could live with.

For Manchester City fans the 1907-08 championship success of their neighbours was a double blow. It was bad enough having to concede the bragging rights to their rivals, but it was exacerbated by the fact that the United team contained several former City stars, sold off cheaply in a fire sale ordered by the FA. Billy Meredith, Sandy Turnbull, Jimmy Bannister and Herbert Burgess were key members of a fine City side that came within a whisker of winning the Double in 1903-04, and were also in the shake-up to win the championship the following year. On the final day of the 1904-05 season City went down at Aston Villa 3-2 in an ill-tempered match. The FA stepped in, but quickly discovered that worse foul play had occurred off the pitch. Meredith was charged with attempting to bribe a Villa player and given a lengthy ban. Further investigations into the club revealed a widespread flouting of the £4-a-week wage cap. City were by no means the only club guilty of making under-the-counter payments, but they were caught with their hands in the till and as an example to others the FA decided on an unprecedented course of action: ordering City to sell off virtually the entire squad. The players were under suspension until 31 December 1906, and City planned to

Fans gather to see the players bring the FA Cup back to Manchester for a second time in 1948. United's first win had been in 1909 when the team defeated Bristol City 1–0 in the final.

hold a grand auction just before the bans were lifted, but the canny Mangnall stole a march on the 34 other League clubs by cutting deals with the men he wanted before the bidding war broke out.

THE 'WELSH WIZARD'
Billy Meredith was a flying winger and one of the game's great showmen, the Bestie of his day. He had already turned 30 when he joined United, but the 'Welsh Wizard' still enjoyed a glittering 15-year spell at the club, and then rejoined City at the ripe old age of 47! Sandy Turnbull – 'Turnbull the Terrible' – was a brilliant inside-forward who top-scored with 25 goals in 30 games in the title-winning season. Unfortunately, he would be embroiled in a further scandal which would sully his own and the club's name before his career was over. Jimmy Bannister was another nifty inside-forward, while full-back Herbert Burgess had been capped four times while playing for City and was regarded as one of the best defenders in the business – especially by Everton, who thought they had agreed a deal to take him to Goodison Park before Mangnall stepped in. Everton's complaint fell on deaf ears at the FA.

The ex-City players weren't the only stars of United's great side of the Edwardian era. The half-back line of Duckworth, Roberts and Bell provided a formidable platform for the silky strikers. Club captain Charlie Roberts, signed from Grimsby in 1904, was an inspirational player, the driving force in the side that would win three major trophies prior to World War One.

He was also outspoken and opinionated, particularly on the subject of the formation of a Players' Union. That belligerent stance is said to have cost him in terms of international appearances, though he did become the first United man to play for England when he took the field at Ayresome Park in a 1-1 draw against Ireland on 25 February 1905. He played in England's next two Home Internationals – both victories – and was then discarded at the age of 22. He extended his illustrious career at Oldham Athletic, whom he also managed, but quit the game to go into the tobacconist business as he found administration no substitute for playing. During his second chosen career he introduced his own brand of cigar, 'Ducrobel', named in honour of the great pre-war United half-back line.

## UNITED WIN INAUGURAL CHARITY SHIELD

United began the 1908-09 campaign by taking a brand new trophy back to Clayton. The inaugural staging of the Charity Shield saw the League champions take on the Southern League winners rather than the Cup holders. United beat Queen's Park Rangers 4-0 at Stamford Bridge in a match that went to a replay, and seven months later added a third piece of silverware to the club's mantelpiece. It wasn't the League championship trophy, for United suffered a dramatic slide down the division, finishing in the bottom half of the table. This season it was to be a different glory trail.

United's record in the FA Cup thus far had been poor, three appearances in the Fourth Round illuminating a path full of early exits. Still, two of those defeats just short of a semi-final berth had come in the last three years – against Woolwich Arsenal in 1905-06 and, against the odds, at the hands of Second division Fulham in the year they took the title – so United were undoubtedly improving as a cup side.

The reigning champions rode their luck on the way to Crystal Palace, the venue for the Final. They were drawn at home for the first three rounds, scraping 1-0 wins against non-league Brighton and Hove Albion and Everton, who would finish that season's championship as runners-up. Then came a 6-1 annihilation of five-time Cup winners Blackburn

Rovers in a one-sided Lancashire derby. Jimmy Turnbull and Sandy Turnbull – no relation – each bagged a hat-trick. The real stroke of good fortune occurred in the quarter-final match at Turf Moor, when the match was abandoned due to a blizzard with the home side 1-0 up and less than 20 minutes to go. United won the rearranged tie 3-2. The semi-final pitted the reigning champions against Newcastle United, the team who would inherit the mantle that year. Newcastle were also Cup holders, but their grasp on the trophy was loosened by a single Harold Halse goal. Having scored the goals that beat Brighton and Everton, Halse did more than his share in helping United realize their Cup dream.

---

Well done, son. United players congratulate 18-year-old Stan Pearson on an outstanding debut at Chesterfield in a Division Two match, 13 November 1937. Salford-born Pearson didn't manage to get on the scoresheet in a seven-goal avalanche but the slick inside-forward skills that would bring him 149 goals over the next 17 years were there from the outset. United secured promotion on the last day of the season, edging out Sheffield United on goal average. The club was back in the top flight, and this time a line was firmly drawn under the lean interwar years.

---

Above: Tickets for the 3rd round cup tie between United and West Brom being sold at the Old Trafford ticket office in January 1939.

Opposite above: After the war, Matt Busby was set to take up a coaching role at Liverpool, the club he had joined in 1936. United scout Louis Rocca urged him to take the top job at United instead. Busby needed little persuading.

## V FOR CUP VICTORY

And so to the final, where Bristol City provided the opposition. They finished in the top half of Division One, five places above United, and would be no push-overs. But having put out the teams that would end the season in first, second and fourth place, United were able to go to Crystal Palace brimming with confidence. A first-half goal from Sandy Turnbull settled the issue in a game that wasn't as close as the score suggests. As both sides played in red, the FA had insisted on a change of colours all round. United opted for an all-white kit with a red V on the shirts; V for victory as it turned out, the first illustrious step along the way to making United the Cup kings of English football. United still had two League games to play, and lost them both in the euphoria of the Cup triumph. But nothing could dampen the spirits of the fans who thronged the streets of Manchester to hail the conquering heroes, a scene that would be repeated ten times in the next 105 years. The story of United's maiden Cup success had one unfortunate footnote, involving the four-legged club mascot. As was customary after a win, the goat in question was given a celebratory drink, but on this joyous occasion the consumption level increased dramatically. By the time the partying was over, a vacancy for a new mascot had arisen.

Four months on from basking in the limelight that attended Cup success, United found themselves a pariah club as the star players engaged in a high-stakes game of brinkmanship with the FA. It revolved round the formation of a Players' Union, which was formed in December 1907 after Billy Meredith chaired a meeting of hundreds of disgruntled footballers keen to assert their rights as employees. There were two bones of contention: the £4-a-week maximum wage, introduced at the turn of the century, and the retain-and-transfer system, which advantaged the clubs at the players' expense. In short, footballers thought they deserved a bigger slice of the cake, and Meredith, along with Charlie Roberts, was at the forefront of the campaign to ensure that they and their fellow professionals were given their due.

## UNITED 'OUTCASTS' TAKE ON FA

The FA refused to recognize the union, and many players buckled under the pressure when contracts were revised to incorporate a clause disavowing the infant collective association. The United hard core would not be intimidated, and the Cup-winning side found itself suspended without pay. With the 1909-10 season a matter of weeks away. Roberts and Co. organized their own training, branding themselves 'Outcasts FC'. That emboldened players from a number of other clubs, and suddenly the FA's autocratic divide-and-rule stance threatened to explode in their faces. At the eleventh hour the authorities relented. The union would be recognized, the suspended players received their back pay and the new season kicked off on schedule.

United finished that historic 1909-10 campaign empty handed: fifth in the League and a Cup exit at the first hurdle. But it was memorable in that the club finally said goodbye and good riddance to Bank Street. In 1908 John Henry Davies had pledged £60,000 to fund a stadium fit for the League champions, and on 19 February 1910 the club's state-of-the-art new Old Trafford home was ready for business. Designed by Archibald Leitch, the

Above: Walter Crickmer, administrator extraordinaire and one of United's greatest servants. As well as being club secretary for over 30 years, Crickmer twice stepped into the breach when United found themselves managerless in the 1930s.

## NEW STADIUM BRINGS CHAMPIONSHIP SUCCESS

Irresistible home form did much to bring United their second championship in 1910-11, the first full campaign launched from Old Trafford. They won 14, drew 4 and lost just once – to Middlesbrough – in their 19 home games that season, though this time it was no romp to the title with a nine-point cushion. In fact, it was out of United's hands on the final day, for Aston Villa were a point clear and had a superior goal average. United needed to beat Sunderland at home and hope Liverpool could do them a favour when they entertained Villa. The fans obviously thought it was a tall order, for Sunderland were riding high and Liverpool were in the bottom half of the table. A sparsely populated Old Trafford witnessed the 5-1 demolition of the Wearsiders, after which news came through that the men from Anfield had fulfilled the other half of the equation. United took the championship by a point.

Many of the players who had triumphed in 1907-08 were still around, including Roberts, Meredith, Halse and 'Turnbull the Terrible'. One new face was striker Enoch West, who had been the League's top marksman the year United won their first championship. Signed from Nottingham Forest in the close season, 'Knocker' weighed in with 19 goals, one more than Turnbull. West was United's top scorer in the next two seasons, too, but the team peaked with that 1910-11 title; there were lean times ahead – and the unpleasant whiff of scandal.

In the summer of 1912 United were rocked by the loss of Ernest Mangnall, the only man other than Sir Matt Busby and Sir Alex Ferguson to bring the League crown to United. Worse still, he crossed the city to join their Hyde Road rivals, whom he served with distinction for over a decade, albeit without the success he enjoyed as United boss. Charlie Roberts soon followed Mangnall out of the Old Trafford door, and United also cashed in on his half-back partner Alex Bell. Trying to balance the books in the years following Old Trafford's construction seemed to take priority over investing in the team.

pre-eminent stadium architect of the day, Old Trafford boasted a gymnasium, billiard room and a 12,000-seat grandstand. Spiralling costs meant the projected 100,000 capacity had to be scaled back, but it was stunning facility for players and fans alike. It also quickly became a fortress that visiting teams found difficult to breach, though United did go down 4-3 to Liverpool in the inaugural fixture.

## UNITED MEN IN BETTING SCAM

United were back in the bottom half of the table by 1913-14, and new manager John Robson must have known the scale of the task facing him. Things got even worse the following season, when relegation-threatened United played out a tame 2-0 home win over mid-table Liverpool at Easter. Bookmakers noticed a flurry of betting activity on that very scoreline – a 7-1 shot – and a match-fixing rat was smelt. An inquiry found three United players and four from Liverpool guilty of collusion, an egregious offence deemed worthy of a life ban for the parties involved. Liverpool's Jackie Sheldon, an ex-United player, was said to be the pivotal figure in the scam. Of the United contingent – Sandy Turnbull, Arthur Whalley and Enoch West – only 'Knocker' took the field against Liverpool. West maintained his innocence, a stance which left the shadow hanging over him for the next 30 years, whereas sterling World War One service wiped the slate clean for the others. Whalley resumed his career when hostilities ended, but for Turnbull it was a posthumous pardon as he was killed in action.

The result of the rigged game was allowed to stand, a vital win as it turned out, for United finished the season one point above the drop zone. Chelsea, in the trapdoor position below them, had every reason to feel aggrieved, but the League was expanded to 22 clubs when football resumed in 1919-20, which serendipitously preserved the London club's top-flight status.

The interwar years were lean ones. Five managers presided over a long fallow period, with secretary Walter Crickmer twice stepping into the breach to help United through an interregnum. Ninth in Division One and an FA Cup semi-final was the best United achieved in that time, those moderate twin peaks both coming in 1925-26, under the stewardship of John Chapman. Shortly afterwards, the FA launched an investigation into United's affairs, as a result of which Chapman was banned from football. The authorities refused to elaborate on the nature of the 'improper conduct' charge of which he was found guilty, and it remains a mystery to this day.

## FANS HOLD CRISIS MEETING

United had three spells in Division Two between the wars, a total of nine years in the second tier. In 1930-31 the team lost their opening 12 games, setting a League record to which they would rather not have laid claim. The Supporters' Club published a plan to turn things round, which went beyond simply calling for the manager's head, though, of course, that was included in the document. When the appeal elicited no response from the board, the fans' mood became more belligerent and there was talk of a mass boycott of the home match against Arsenal on 18 October. Thousands attended a meeting at Hulme Town Hall to discuss the issue the day before the game, and the gate for the Gunners' visit was indeed well below expectation. The 23,000 who turned up witnessed defeat number eleven. That figure dropped to 4,000 when United entertained Middlesbrough in the final game of a wretched season. They finished the campaign nine points adrift of the field, and another manager was soon on his way, though the reason for Herbert Bamlett's departure was rather more transparent than Chapman's.

Spare a thought for Joe Spence, one of United's immortals, who played over 500 games for the club when it was adrift in the doldrums. 'Give it to Joe,' was a regular cry from the terraces, unsurprisingly, since Spence's dazzling wing play was one of precious few highlights in an inauspicious 20-year period. He was the club's top scorer on seven occasions and held United's appearance record until Bill Foulkes raised the bar in the 1960s. Spence must have treasured his two England caps, for he had no club honours to show for his outstanding contribution over a 14-year period.

If results on the pitch weren't bad enough, the situation was exacerbated by an extremely unhealthy balance sheet. By the early 1930s the club was staring into the abyss, a financial crisis comparable with the last days of the Newton Heath regime. Crippling interest payments and falling gate receipts meant bankruptcy was again a real possibility, and there was no John Henry Davies to bale them out; United's chairman and great benefactor for a generation had died in 1927. A new messiah with deep pockets was needed, and, right on cue, one turned up.

## THE NEW MESSIAH

James W Gibson was a clothing magnate who, like Davies 30 years earlier, learned of United's plight by a circuitous route and was prepared to invest heavily – as long as he be allowed to call the tune from the boardroom. The directors had little choice. The banks had turned off the credit tap and there was no money to pay the players, let alone bring in new blood. In the spring of 1932 Manchester United had a new chairman.

The injection of funds didn't have an immediate effect, not least because the first managerial appointment under the Gibson regime, Scott Duncan, failed to live up to his impressive billing. In fact, United reached their nadir in 1933-34, when the spectre of relegation to the Third Division loomed large. United

---

Opposite below: The team line up in the 1938–1939 season. Back row left-right: Brown, Roughton, Breedon, Manley, Breen, McKay, Baird. Sitting left-right: B. Inglis, (Assistant Trainer), Bryant, Craven, Smith, J. Griffiths, Vose, T. Curry (Trainer). Front left-right: Redwood, Gladwin and Pearson.

Below: United's blitzed Old Trafford stadium in 1945.

went into the Lions' Den of Millwall on the last day of the season for a winner-take-all battle. A draw would have favoured Millwall, who went into the match a point ahead of United, but the visitors came away with a 2-0 victory. Duncan did guide United back to the First Division in 1935-36, but a year later they were plying their trade in the second tier again. The false dawn came at a particularly inopportune moment: it occurred as Manchester City celebrated winning the championship, having twice been to Wembley earlier in the decade. On the field representing the blue half of Manchester in those two FA Cup showpieces was a certain Matt Busby.

Busby was born in 1909, the year of United's first Cup success. He joined City as a 17-year-old inside-forward, but struggled to make the first team and considered quitting the game. By 1930 City were prepared to sell, and United were said to be interested, though the Old Trafford coffers wouldn't run to the £150 asking price. The turning point in Busby's fortunes came when he filled in at wing-half in a Third XI game. By accident he had found his best position, and was soon a first-team regular in the half-back line. He won his sole cap for Scotland – war internationals apart – in a 3-2 defeat by Wales at Ninian Park in the 1933 Home International

---

Below: Charlie Mitten hits the back of the net in a warm-up friendly prior to the start of the 1946-47 season. Like all teams, United had to assess the strength of its playing staff when League football returned after a seven-year hiatus, to see which of those on the books could still cut the mustard in the professional game. Busby was luckier than some, for he inherited a strong nucleus: 'keeper Jack Crompton, full backs Johnny Carey and John Aston, a formidable half-back line comprising Henry Cockburn, Allenby Chilton and Jack Warner, plus four forwards any manager would have liked in his side: Jack Rowley, Stan Pearson, Johnny Morris – and Mitten himself. All except Crompton and Mitten would gain international honours.

championship. Facing Busby that day was Jimmy Murphy, though it wasn't until their paths crossed during their time in the Services that the two became firm friends.

## BUSBY JOINS 'OTHER' REDS

Having played with distinction for one of United's great rivals, Busby joined another traditional foe in March 1936. His £8000 move to Anfield came at a time when Liverpool were an average side, though, unlike United, they managed to steer clear of relegation. In 1938-39, the last season before the enforced eight-year hiatus, Busby helped Liverpool to 11th place in the League. United, who had just won promotion on goal average, by a wafer-thin margin, announced their return to the big time by finishing 14th. The war effectively ended Busby's playing days – he had turned 30 by the time he swapped his football kit for army uniform. His thoughts were already turning towards finding a niche within the game after hanging up his boots, and to that end his current employers were keen to offer him a job on the Anfield coaching staff.

United, meanwhile, were soldiering on with Walter Crickmer again in charge, Duncan having resigned early in the 1937-38 season. The need for a permanent manager was pressing, and scout Louis Rocca – the man credited with naming the baby when Manchester United was born 40 years earlier – joined the hunt for Busby's signature. The two had struck up a friendship when Rocca tried to broker the deal to bring the £150 City reject to Old Trafford. United missed out on acquiring the services of Busby the player; Rocca was determined that the club shouldn't make the same mistake with Busby the manager.

The challenge for the new incumbent was enormous. The ground was a bomb-site, courtesy of the Luftwaffe, and the club was £15,000 in the red. But the prospect of a return to Manchester to take charge of an archetypal sleeping giant was irresistible. He demanded – and got – a five-year contract, and set about the task of building the legend.

## PART ONE

# Busby sets the stage

# 'Brittle Bones' gamble pays off handsomely

**Bottom:** The first great side of the post-war era, assembled for the princely sum of £7750. Jack Rowley and Johnny Carey, acquired for £3500 and £250 respectively, were already on United's books when Busby took over the managerial reins. His first major signing was winger Jimmy Delaney, who arrived from Celtic early in 1946 in a £4000 deal. This was an era when teams invariably played with a five-man forward line, and with Rowley, Mitten, Pearson and Morris already on the staff, Busby targeted Delaney as the man to complete his attack. At 31 and with an injury record that had earned him the sobriquet 'Brittle Bones', Delaney was seen as something of a gamble. It paid off handsomely, however, Delaney giving invaluable service for four seasons, helping United become regular title contenders and lift the Cup for the first time in 39 years. 'It was like fitting the last piece in the jigsaw,' said club captain Johnny Carey of the man who completed an exciting attacking line-up that was dubbed the Famous Five. Back row (l to r) Delaney, Warner, Pearson, Crompton, Rowley, Lynn, Chilton. Front row (l to r) Morris, Anderson, Carey, Aston, Cockburn and Mitten.

**Above left:** Johnny Carey, a true Captain Marvel for his exploits all over the pitch – including goalkeeper!

**Middle left:** Half-back John Anderson played just 39 games for United, five of those in the glorious 1947–48 FA Cup run. His goal at Wembley against Blackpool was one of only two he scored in a United shirt.

**Above right:** Johnny Carey, pictured at his wedding.

**Above middle and below left:** Jack Rowley, star striker of the early postwar years.

**Above:** United's stalwart 'keeper Jack Crompton snuffs out a Blackpool attack in the 1948 Cup Final, gathering the ball ahead of England international Stan Mortensen. United and Blackpool had both hit 18 goals en route to the final, and those hoping for a high-scoring Wembley classic were not disappointed. Crompton made a crucial save from Mortensen

---

### Busby's first major signing was winger Jimmy Delaney, who arrived from Celtic in a £4000 deal.

---

when the score was 2–2, and it was his smart clearance that led to Stan Pearson putting United ahead for the first time in the match. A deflected shot from half-back John Anderson ensured that the Cup was heading to Old Trafford for the second time in the club's history. Success brought its own problems as ageing squad members demanded a bigger slice of the

cake to try to cash in during their twilight years in the professional game. It wouldn't be the last time that Busby had to face dissenting voices in the ranks, and on each occasion he acted decisively, even if it involved shipping a talented player out of the door. The first big name to discover that the smooth running of the club was more important than any individual was inside-forward Johnny Morris. He hit 21 goals in 1947–48 but that didn't stop Busby selling him to Derby for a record £24,500 the following season, after the player questioned the manager's decision to leave him out of the side. Some of the squad initially thought the manager's action might have cost United the chance of a return visit to Wembley – they lost to Wolves in the semis – but they eventually saw its wisdom. Morris went on to play for England, but Busby firmly demonstrated that cohesion was a vital ingredient for a club's success.

**Left:** Jimmy Delaney in action against Charlton at the Valley March 1949. United won 3–2.

# Busby acts to quash dissenting voice

United take
the hard road
to Cup victory

Right: Jack Rowley soars to meet a corner early in the 1948 FA Cup Final. His aerial power eventually paid off, the second of his two goals coming from a spectacular diving header. Given his scoring record, Rowley was unlucky not to earn greater international honours, though he did notch up six goals in as many appearances in an England shirt. Unfortunately, Rowley was up against some stiff competition with the likes of Lawton, Mortensen and Milburn on the scene. Rowley scored his 208th and final goal for United in January 1955, by which time Tommy Taylor had taken the No. 9 shirt. He may have been one of United's greatest ever strikers, but, incredibly, Rowley wasn't even the hotshot of his own family: brother Arthur eclipsed Jack's prodigious scoring achievements, netting a league record 434 goals in his career.

Above: Johnny Carey is hoisted aloft after United's 4–2 Cup Final victory over Blackpool. United's second success in the competition came 39 years to the day after the first, a 1–0 win over Bristol City in 1909. They did it the hard way this time, becoming the first club in history to face First Division opposition in every round. Aston Villa were the first victims, followed by reigning league champions Liverpool, Charlton Athletic, Preston and Derby en route to Wembley. All except Charlton would finish in the top half of the table. A further handicap was the fact that United were on the road every step of the way, and not just to their 'second home' Maine Road, where United played their fixtures while Old Trafford was out of commission. United's three 'home' Cup ties were played on days when City needed their stadium, forcing Busby's men to become nomads. The final was a classic, one for the purist, but the most dramatic tie was the Third Round trip to Villa Park. United found themselves a goal down inside 15 seconds, but by half-time they were sitting on a 5–1 lead. Villa fought back to 5–4 before United added a sixth.

The club had to pay £5000 per annum plus a share of the gate receipts for the privilege of using Maine Road.

# Mitten nets first Old Trafford goal for eight years

This page: Charlie Mitten had been on United's books for 10 years before making his debut at the age of 25 at the start of the 1946–47 season. His dashing wing play made him a huge crowd favourite over the next four years, and he got an extra special roar after scoring the first post-war goal at Old Trafford, on 24 August 1949. It ended an eight-year 'homeless' period, following the damage to the ground by German bombers in March 1941. It also boosted United's coffers, for the club had had to pay £5000 per annum plus a share of the gate receipts for the privilege of using Maine Road. Mitten's best personal haul came in March 1950, when he scored four in a 7–0 thrashing United handed out to Villa at Old Trafford, three of them from the penalty spot. When he placed the ball for the third spot-kick, Villa 'keeper Joe Rutherford enquired which corner Mitten was planning to put the ball in. 'Same as the other two,' came the reply, and Mitten coolly slotted home.

# 'Nearly' men for third year running

Left: 16 October 1948. Jack Crompton clutches a high ball and makes sure there are no scraps for Stoke City centre-forward Steele to feed off. United went down 2–1 in this league encounter at the Victoria Ground. The team that had won the Cup and finished second in the league the previous campaign made an indifferent start to the 1948–49 season, the Stoke result one of five defeats in the opening 13 matches. Busby's men then put a run together, losing only one of the next 16, and rounding off the campaign with four straight wins. It wasn't quite enough to catch champions Portsmouth, but runners-up for the third year running – to a different club on each occasion – showed a remarkable level of consistency. It could so easily have been a repeat performance of 1947–48 – second in the league and Cup winners – but in the latter competition United were edged out 1–0 by Wolves in the semis, a tie that went to a replay. Had they come through that match, Division Two strugglers Leicester City were waiting in the final, and Wolves brushed them aside comfortably in the Wembley showpiece.

---

**Jack Rowley hit the back of the net 30 times in 40 games during the 1951–52 season.**

---

Below left: Jack Rowley and Johnny Carey were both the wrong side of 30 when the 1951–52 season got under way. Having been part of a team that had finished runner-up four times in five years, they might have thought their chance of a championship medal had gone. But the goal ace and club captain finally got their hands on the medal they richly deserved. Rowley hit the back of the net 30 times in 40 games, almost one-third of United's 95-goal tally, while Carey weighed in with three in his 38 league appearances.

# Defensive rock
# sets appearance record

This page: Allenby Chilton was a rock at the heart of United's defence in Busby's first great side of the postwar era. He chalked up almost 400 appearances for the club, including a run of 166 consecutive league matches, which remained a club record until Steve Coppell cracked the 200 mark in the early 1980s. Chilton's achievement was remarkable for a player who made his debut as a 20-year-old on the day before Britain entered World War II. Had he not been robbed of seven league campaigns, Chilton would surely have been near the top of the appearance chart in the club's annals. And had Billy Wright and Neil Franklin not formed a mighty defensive axis at the heart of England's defence, Chilton might have had more than two caps to show for his outstanding career. Like Busby, Chilton had been on Liverpool's books, albeit for a brief spell as an amateur. He joined United in November 1938 and was still going strong in the 1954–55 season, at the age of 36, when he was supplanted by rising star Mark Jones. Realizing there was no way back, Chilton left Old Trafford to take over as player-manager of Grimsby Town a month after losing his first-team place.

# 'Gunner' snatched from under Wolves' nose

**Left:** United trio John Aston, Jack Rowley and Henry Cockburn limber up for England's match against Sweden in Stockholm, 13 May 1949, where Walter Winterbottom's side went down 3–1. Aston and Cockburn both began their careers as inside-forwards but Busby switched them to great effect. Cockburn became part of a marvellous half-back line, playing alongside Allenby Chilton and Jack Warner. Aston was converted into a left-back, a trick the manager repeated with both Johnny Carey and Roger Byrne. Busby's keenness to have ball-playing defenders was revolutionary at a time when the norm was for rugged stoppers. Aston and his son, John Jnr, both won a championship medal with United, and both tasted cup success. Aston Snr played in the FA Cup-winning side of 1948, while his flying winger son starred in the 1968 European Cup triumph. Dad had the edge when it came to the international stage, winning two of his 17 caps at the 1950 World Cup. Unfortunately, one of those was the infamous 1–0 defeat against the USA in Belo Horizonte, widely regarded as the low point in the history of the international team.

**Below left:** Jack Rowley relaxing at his Sale home with wife Violet and their two children in 1949. 'Gunner' Rowley scored four goals in only his second appearance for United, against Swansea in autumn 1937, when he was just 17. A goal every other game over the next 17 years was a fantastic return on the £3000 United paid Bournemouth for his services. Rowley had been on the books of his local club, Wolves, but slipped through the Molineux net without making a senior appearance. It was his goalscoring exploits on the south coast that brought a number of scouts running, with United boss Scott Duncan winning the race for his signature. Duncan was a beleaguered figure, having presided over five years of mediocrity. His time was nearly up, the signing of Rowley one of his final acts as United manager. But in recruiting Rowley, along with the teenage Johnny Carey, Duncan had bequeathed to his postwar successor Matt Busby two wonderful gifts.

# Busby builds on thriving nursery set-up

Top right and bottom left: John Aston was a one-club man, giving sterling service for eight years following his debut in September 1946. He once fractured an arm in a game and played on the wing wearing a sling. In the pre-substitutes' era it wasn't unusual to see the walking wounded out on the flanks. Aston signed off at the end of the 1953–54 season, by which time several of the 'Babes' had made their debuts and others were knocking on the door. Although Busby firmly believed in the maxim 'if you're good enough, you're old enough', he didn't have to develop a youth policy from scratch when he arrived at Old Trafford, for there was a thriving junior set-up already in place. Manchester United Junior Athletic Club – of which Aston was a graduate – was formed in 1938 as a nursery team, its players recruited following exhaustive scouting missions. The template may have been established seven years before Busby took over, but he took the business of unearthing young talent to a new level. The crop of youngsters that came through United's ranks in the 1950s remained unrivalled until 'Fergie's Fledglings' carried all before them 40 years later.

> **The crop of youngsters that came through United's ranks in the 1950s remained unrivalled until 'Fergie's Fledglings'.**

Middle: John Aston and Stan Pearson hope that Sunderland 'keeper Mapson is going to spill the ball during a League match at Old Trafford on 26 December 1950. It was Boxing Day gloom as United went down 5–3, having lost to the same opposition at Roker Park 24 hours earlier. Coming on top of a home defeat by Bolton on 23 December, it meant a miserable Christmas for United fans – three losses in four days – though Busby's men still finished second in the title race.
Top left: Henry Cockburn in April 1948.
Bottom right: Busby splashed out a club record £18,000 to bring John Downie from Bradford Park Avenue in March 1949, as replacement for the departed Johnny Morris. It represented excellent business, for the coffers had been swelled by £24,500 from the sale of Morris. More important than the £6000 Busby had made on the deals was the fact that he had lost a troublemaker and gained a team player.

# 'Nobody stops the ball except the goalkeeper'

**Right:** Jack Crompton fends off a robust challenge from Smyth of Wolves in the FA Cup semi-final at Hillsborough, 26 March 1949. The game ended in a 1–1 draw, but the men from Molineux loosened the holders' grip on the trophy in the replay. Busby was scornful of the power game and direct football, of which Wolves became the arch exponents over the next decade. He favoured the 'pass and move' style, summed up in one of his favourite mantras: 'Nobody stops the ball except the goalkeeper.'

**Middle:** Crompton makes a spectacular save in the FA Cup semi-final replay at Goodison Park. Under Stan Cullis, Wolves vied with United not only in the First Division but in the junior ranks. The two clubs contested the first two finals of the Youth Cup after the competition was instituted in 1952–53. Like Busby, Cullis prided himself on the Molineux scouting system, which must have made it particularly galling when the Reds snatched Dudley-born Duncan Edwards from under their rival's nose. Edwards supported Wolves as a boy and was training regularly at Molineux. But no club could sign a youngster until the age of 15, and by then Duncan was so smitten by the panache of Busby's side that he only ever wanted to go to Old Trafford.

**Below:** 'Gentleman' Johnny Carey tackles Huddersfield winger Vic Metcalfe – from behind, but perfectly legally at the time – in a league match at Old Trafford, 5 November 1949. United ran riot, the dynamic duo Rowley and Pearson scoring twice each in a 6–0 win. It wasn't the team's best result of the season – Aston Villa were hit with a seven-goal blitz later in the season – but United slipped to fourth in the championship. Busby's first great side was ageing, but there was to be one final hurrah before it had to be disbanded.

Busby was scornful of the power game and direct football, favouring instead the 'pass and move' style.

# Busby shows 'Bogota Bandit' the door

Right: Charlie Mitten challenges Fulham 'keeper Kelly during a league match at Craven Cottage, 10 December 1949. United slipped to only their third defeat of the season, and would go on to finish fourth, three points adrift of champions Portsmouth. Although United would finish runners-up and champions themselves in the next two seasons, many feel that Busby's first great side peaked with the 1948 FA Cup victory over Blackpool. Mitten was a key member of that side, but left Old Trafford under a cloud a year before the Reds claimed their first league title under Busby. United fans were shocked when their star winger followed a cash trail that led to Colombian side Santa Fe in 1950. Offers of £40 a week when the maximum wage in English football was pegged at £12 lured several players to South America, but it proved to be a mirage, and Mitten was soon back at Old Trafford with his tail between his legs. The FA slapped a £250 fine and a six-month suspension on the 'Bogota Bandit', as he was dubbed, and Busby was equally unforgiving. Mitten was soon on his way, sold to Fulham for £20,000. He was the only member of United's 'Famous Five' attack not to be capped, his cause not helped by defection to a country beyond Fifa's jurisdiction.

Middle left: Like Denis Law, Henry Cockburn was spring-heeled when it came to aerial battles, capable of outjumping much taller opponents.

Middle right: Despite the six-year interruption to his career caused by the war, Stan Pearson made a total of 346 appearances for United.

Below right: Young Mark Jones bulks up with a hearty breakfast to ensure his place in the United first team. The pipe-smoking gentle giant vied for the No. 5 shirt with Jackie Blanchflower. Both were outstanding centre-halves, though with differing strengths. Jones was a commanding stopper, dominant in the air, while Blanchflower had the edge in the skills department. The Irishman got the nod for the 1957 FA Cup Final and was the man in possession until just before Munich, when Jones was restored to the side.

Below left: Stan Pearson hooks the ball off the toe of a Portsmouth defender in a top-of-the-table clash at Old Trafford during the run-in to the 1949–50 season. United were in the middle of a nine-match winless streak which wasn't ended until the final game, by which time all hope of a third league title had gone.

> In the first 15 seasons of postwar football, United averaged 85.4 in the 'Goals For' column, conceding 59.2.

# United revel in cavalier approach of postwar era

Top: 4 March 1950. Jack Crompton fails to keep out a drive by Chelsea's Roy Bentley in an FA Cup Sixth Round clash at Stamford Bridge. It put Chelsea 2–0 up, which is how the game ended. Having put out a Portsmouth side that would go on to win the championship for the second year running in the previous round, United must have fancied their chances against mid-table Chelsea, but any hopes of a third FA Cup win were dashed by the England centre-forward. An important victory had been won, however: retaining Matt Busby's services as manager. Busby turned down an offer to take over at White Hart Lane in 1949, Spurs eventually appointing Arthur Rowe. Rowe's 'push-and-run' side played the same brand of stylish football as United, and after running away with the

Division Two championship, they pipped the Reds for the league crown in 1950–51. United had their revenge the following year, and this time it was Spurs who had to settle for the runner-up spot.

Above: Highbury, 14 October 1950. An unruffled Johnny Carey clears a goalbound ball with 'keeper Reg Allen and Arsenal's Don Roper spectators on the deck. Allen was in his debut season, having signed from QPR that summer for £11,000, a British record fee for a goalkeeper. He was beaten three times that day, the 3–0 defeat one of 10 reverses in the 1950–51 league campaign. Even so, United went on to finish runners-up for the fourth time in five years. It was an era when a double-digit figure in the losses column was the norm, even for teams at the top of the table. In

the first six postwar seasons there were just seven instances of a club keeping the number of defeats to single figures. United achieved it on three occasions, Spurs, Wolves, Portsmouth and Arsenal each managing it once. The United side that took the title in 1951–52 lost eight of their 42 games, conceding 52 goals. That was four goals more than United shipped in the relegation season of 1973–74. On the other hand, the class of 1951–52 found the net 95 times – 57 more than Doc's side managed when it went down. United typified the 'we'll-score-more-than-you' philosophy of the postwar period. In the first 15 seasons after league football resumed, United averaged 85.4 in the 'Goals For' column, conceding 59.2.

Below and bottom right: John Aston on the field in 1951 and off the field with his family (right). Watching him mend a boot is his son, the future United player, John Aston Junior.

Bottom left: Arsenal goalkeeper Swindin prepares to save a flying header from United's John Downie. Downie's name may not be as familiar to United fans as Tommy Taylor and Denis Law, or, indeed, Bryan Robson, Andy Cole and Rio Ferdinand. Yet in their time all have held the tag of United's most expensive acquisition. Downie kept that dubious honour for four years, until Busby raised the mark substantially in order to persuade Barnsley to part with goal ace Tommy Taylor.

**Left:** Headshots of Stan Pearson (above) and Johnny Berry (below).
**Below:** Aston scores United's first goal against Chelsea at Stamford Bridge in December 1952. Aston showed his remarkable versatility that season, full-back one week, leading the attack the next. His goal at Chelsea continued a hot scoring streak – eight in ten games – during a mid-season spell wearing the No. 9 shirt. United won the game 3-2, the other two goals coming from inside-forward John Doherty on one of his rare first team outings.
**Above:** Chelsea's Roy Bentley challenges Crompton for the ball during United's FA Cup sixth round tie against Chelsea at Stamford Bridge in 1950.

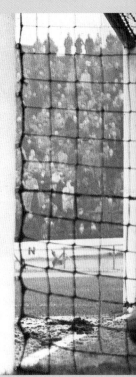

# Troublemakers shape Busby vision

Below: Matt Busby gives his squad and backroom team a leisurely pep talk. Jimmy Murphy is on the front row, far right, while Tom Curry and Bert Whalley are at the back, right and fourth from right respectively. Also on the back row, second from left, is iron-man centre-half Allenby Chilton. His mood appears relaxed here, but on one occasion in the early days of Busby's tenure when the side was underperforming, Chilton stood up and took over the team talk. There was a mere nine-year age gap between manager and player, which perhaps gave the latter the courage to speak his mind, especially as win bonuses were at stake. Run-ins of this kind no doubt helped shape Busby's vision: to scour the land for a crop of talented, more malleable youngsters that he could mould into a team of world-beaters. Right: Taking it easy on the deck of the USA-bound Queen Mary after the exertions of the 1949–50 season, in which United finished fourth in the League and reached the last eight of the Cup. Right to left: John Ball, Charlie Mitten, Jack Warner, Tom Lowrie, Jimmy Delaney, Allenby Chilton, Brian Birch, Tom McNulty, Johnny Carey, Henry Cockburn, Stan Pearson, Jack Crompton, Johnny Downie, Tommy Bogan, Sammy Lynn, club secretary

Walter Crickmer, Jack Rowley. Downie had become United's record buy when he signed from Second Division Bradford Park Avenue for £18,000 the previous year as replacement for perceived troublemaker Johnny Morris. Busby would up the record three times in his 25 years in charge, paying Barnsley £29,999 for Tommy Taylor in 1953, £45,000 to bring Albert Quixall from Sheffield Wednesday in 1958 and £115,000 to end Denis Law's Serie A nightmare with Torino in 1962.

# United hit Gunners for six in title showdown

**Right:** Allenby Chilton was a key member of Busby's first great side, Division One runners-up four times in five years before taking the championship in 1951–52. With six defeats by mid-November, United looked like heading for another season of disappointment. But from that point on the team was almost irresistible. They lost just twice in the remaining 24 league games to finish four points clear of Spurs and Arsenal. The Gunners came to Old Trafford on the last day of the season with a theoretical chance of snatching the title. Joe Mercer's side needed to win by seven goals, a task made even less likely when they went down to 10 men midway through the first half. United ran riot, Rowley bagging a hat-trick in a 6–1 win. The league crown was back at Old Trafford for the third time, following the two championship successes of the Edwardian era.

# 'Gentleman Johnny' dons every shirt except No.11

**Below:** The great postwar side was skippered by Johnny Carey, one of the most extraordinary players ever to pull on a football shirt. Snapped up for just £250 after being spotted playing in Dublin, Carey joined United in November 1936. The newspaper hoardings announced the club's latest star acquisition – only for Carey to discover they referred to inside-forward Ernie Thomson, who signed from Blackburn at the same time, for 18 times Carey's fee! Thomson turned out just three times for United; Carey served the club somewhat better. Over the next 17 years 'Gentleman John' played 344 games, despite the loss of seven years to the global conflict. Carey was Mr Versatile, turning out in every position bar outside-left, performing heroics even when pressed into goalkeeping service in a 2–2 draw at Sunderland in February 1953. He was capped 29 times for the Republic of Ireland, and his distinguished war service rendered him eligible for international honours north of the border too. In September 1946 Carey faced England twice in three days, first on the wrong end of a 7–2 defeat for Northern Ireland in Belfast, then turning out for Eire in Dublin, when the result was the same though the scoreline was a more respectable 1–0. In 1949, the year he picked up the Footballer of the Year award, Carey captained the Republic side that inflicted a 2–0 defeat on England at Goodison Park. This came four years before Hungary's famous demolition job at Wembley, and marked England's first true home defeat by 'overseas' opposition. Carey was offered a place on the Board when he hung up his boots, the minutes honouring a man who had 'covered his career with glory and set a shining example to all who follow him', but he chose to go into coaching and management, beginning his new career with Blackburn Rovers.

# Playing through the pain barrier

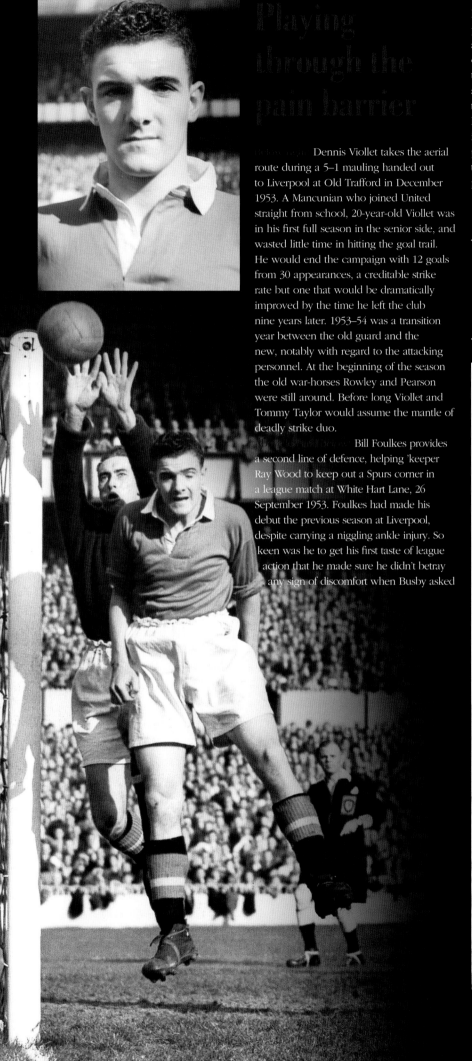

Dennis Viollet takes the aerial route during a 5–1 mauling handed out to Liverpool at Old Trafford in December 1953. A Mancunian who joined United straight from school, 20-year-old Viollet was in his first full season in the senior side, and wasted little time in hitting the goal trail. He would end the campaign with 12 goals from 30 appearances, a creditable strike rate but one that would be dramatically improved by the time he left the club nine years later. 1953–54 was a transition year between the old guard and the new, notably with regard to the attacking personnel. At the beginning of the season the old war-horses Rowley and Pearson were still around. Before long Viollet and Tommy Taylor would assume the mantle of deadly strike duo.

Bill Foulkes provides a second line of defence, helping 'keeper Ray Wood to keep out a Spurs corner in a league match at White Hart Lane, 26 September 1953. Foulkes had made his debut the previous season at Liverpool, despite carrying a niggling ankle injury. So keen was he to get his first taste of league action that he made sure he didn't betray any sign of discomfort when Busby asked him to jump and land on the injured leg prior to the match. It was a high-risk strategy as Foulkes was up against Billy Liddell, idol of the Anfield terraces. Liddell did score, though United won the match 2–1. Foulkes soon made the right back spot his own, though he suspected that he hadn't fooled his manager for one moment. This was no isolated incident. Busby expected his men to play through the pain barrier, and such was their commitment to him and the club, the players were only too willing to do so.

> ## Before long Viollet and Tommy Taylor would assume the mantle of deadly strike duo.

# Winless streak spurs Busby into action

**Left:** John Aston in action early in the 1953–54 season, which United began with an eight-match winless streak. Although the team still managed to finish fourth – an improvement on the previous campaign – Busby saw the need for radical change to put United back at the top of the league. Aston was just one of the veterans whose days were numbered.

**Below:** Ray Wood signed from Darlington as an 18-year-old in 1949, but had to bide his time while Jack Crompton and Reg Allen vied for the goalkeeping jersey before he took over as first choice between the sticks in 1954–55. Wood had lightning reflexes and was a fine shot stopper, and had he been more adept at dealing with crosses, he would surely have won more international honours. The £5000 fee United paid for Wood turned out to be excellent business as Wood clocked up over 200 games in his nine years at the club. Tommy Taylor and Johnny Berry were the only other members of the side that won back-to-back championships in 1955–56 and 1956–57 to join for a fee, and the aggregate cost of those three transfers was just £50,000.

**Below left:** Wood takes to the training pitch with the England squad – including Roger Byrne – prior to a Wembley clash with Wales, 10 November 1954. Both United stars played in the 3–2 victory, Wood winning his second cap in as many internationals. The selectors tried several other 'keepers before Wood made his third and final appearance in an England shirt, in a 5–1 win over Finland in May 1956. At least his brief international career ended with a 100 per cent record: three wins, 10 goals scored, three conceded.

# Old guard make way for young stars

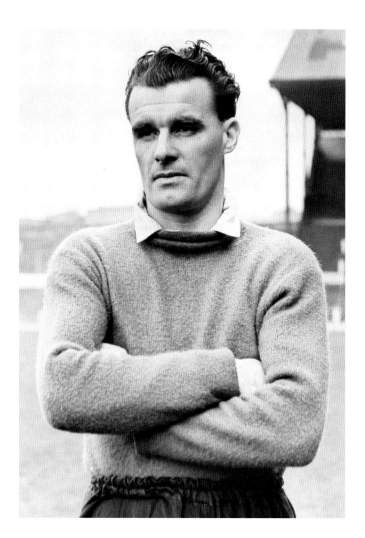

Left: Out with the old: Stan Pearson ended his glorious 17-year United career with a move to Bury in February 1954. Thirty-four-year-old Pearson had begun the 1953–54 season as the new club captain, stepping into the sizeable boots vacated by Johnny Carey. He scored United's goal in the opening game, a 1–1 home draw against Chelsea, but sustained an injury which signalled the beginning of the end. Pearson had another brief run in the side that autumn, but intense competition for places in the forward line meant that he had to look elsewhere for first-team action. His departure left Jack Rowley as the only member of the 'Famous Five' still on United's books, though a year later the 'Gunner' also called time on his United career. Both Pearson and Rowley tried their hand at management, the latter having a spell as Ajax boss in the early 1960s, just before Rinus Michels turned the Amsterdam club into world beaters with his Total Football philosophy. Rowley and Pearson, who had terrorized defences in a deadly strike partnership, died within a year of each other in the late 1990s.

Below: In with the new: one of the men who hastened Pearson's exit was Jackie Blanchflower, who became a first-team regular in the forward line that season. Blanchflower had already turned out at half-back, and would go on to give assured performances in central defence, making him the most versatile performer of the era, along with Johnny Carey and Duncan Edwards.

# Crowds flock to watch tyros' goal-fest

Above: The Lord and Lady Mayoress of Manchester present David Pegg with the winners' trophy after United's success in an international youth tournament staged in Switzerland in 1954. United were unbeaten, scoring 21 goals in their seven matches. On the domestic front, Busby's young tyros had just retained the FA Youth Cup, beating Wolves in the final for the second year running. United would record five consecutive wins from 1953 to 1957, attracting crowds averaging over 20,000 at Old Trafford. It was hardly surprising, as the team entertained them royally, hitting 33 goals in the 10 games of those two-legged finals.

Right and opposite below left: Mark Jones gained his regular place in the team during the 1956-57 season when Allenby Chilton was transferred to Grimsby.

Opposite below right: United's 1954–55 championship hopes were dealt a blow over the Christmas period when they lost to Aston Villa on consecutive days. Here, Villa 'keeper Keith Jones foils a United attack at Villa Park on 28 December, the home side running out 2–1 winners. The previous day United had been beaten 1–0 at Old Trafford. The two teams had identical records at the end of the season, United taking fifth place on goal average. But the clubs were moving in different directions: the following season Villa avoided relegation by a whisker while United romped to the league title.

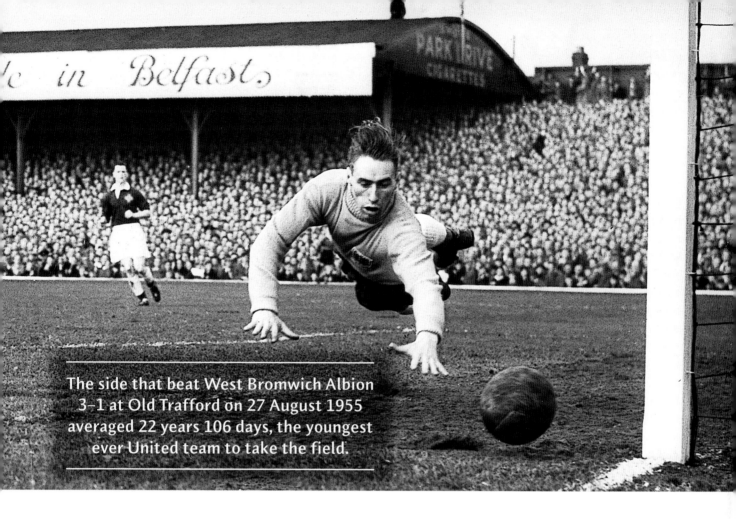

The side that beat West Bromwich Albion 3–1 at Old Trafford on 27 August 1955 averaged 22 years 106 days, the youngest ever United team to take the field.

# Busby fields youngest ever United side

**Above:** United players in opposition. Ray Wood saves from Northern Ireland's Jackie Blanchflower, with Roger Byrne on hand to deal with any rebound during an international staged at Windsor Park, Belfast, 2 October 1954. Bill Foulkes, one of the prostrate group looking on, was winning his first England cap, as was Wood. England won the game 2–0 with goals from Johnny Haynes and Don Revie. Busby was still feeding his Youth Team stars into the senior side, the average age of the team falling with each promotion. The side that beat West Bromwich Albion 3–1 at Old Trafford on 27 August 1955 averaged 22 years 106 days, the youngest ever United team to take the field. The trend was set to continue as teenagers Eddie Colman and David Pegg were about to become first-team regulars. The 'old man' of the side was 26-year-old skipper Roger Byrne.

**Below middle:** Dennis Violett is denied a goal by Chelsea 'keeper Bill Robertson and centre half Ron Greenwood. The league match, played at Stamford Bridge on 16 October 1954, resulted in a 6–5 victory for United.

# England selectors ignore Viollet-Taylor partnership

Above right: Dennis Viollet in action at Stamford Bridge, 16 October 1954. The United goal ace bagged a hat-trick in a remarkable 6–5 victory, with Tommy Taylor grabbing two. Viollet and Taylor formed a lethal strike partnership, which brought an avalanche of goals before Munich claimed Taylor's life. In 1955–56, the year of the Babes' first championship success, only in half a dozen league games when both men took the field did the scoresheet fail to register either a Viollet or a Taylor goal. If ever there was a case for replicating a club pairing at international level, this was it. Yet while Taylor was elevated to the England ranks within weeks of signing for United, and went on to hit a phenomenal 16 goals in 19 games for his country, Viollet was capped just twice, both times after Taylor had lost his life at Munich. He got on the scoresheet in his second outing, a 4–1 victory over Luxembourg in a World Cup qualifier in 1961, but was never picked again.
Below middle: Johnny Berry, who, along with Roger Byrne, was the only first-team regular in all three championship-winning sides of the 1950s. Berry arrived at Old Trafford when the 1951–52 season was a few games old. Busby had faced a tricky problem. He began the campaign with a team capable of winning the league, except for an obvious lack in the wing

department. Charlie Mitten and Jimmy Delaney had gone, and the players he had tried in their stead – including Harry McShane, father of actor Ian – hadn't quite come off. Time wasn't on Busby's side, so he dipped into the coffers for Berry, bought from Birmingham City for £25,000. Some 52 years before Alex Ferguson signed Cristiano Ronaldo after the Portuguese ran his defenders ragged in a friendly against Sporting Lisbon, Busby acquired Berry for exactly the same reason. Berry had caught the eye with some dazzling wing play in recent United–Birmingham encounters, notably in April 1950, when he scored at Old Trafford in a 2–0 win for the visitors.
Bottom: Manchester United's Tommy Taylor was bought from Barnsley by Matt Busby for

£1 short of £30,000 to avoid burdening him. 26 goals in 44 games brought convoys of scouts to Oakwell, and a string of clubs were said to be after Taylor's signature. Within two months of arriving at Old Trafford, he picked up his first cap, against Argentina in Buenos Aires, 17 May 1953. That was a brief outing as the match was abandoned after 20 minutes due to a waterlogged pitch. Taylor opened his England account in his first full match, a 2-1 win against Chile a week later. His strike partner that day was Nat Lofthouse, the man who would dash United's Cup hopes in 1958, three months after Taylor lost his life at Munich.

> Berry had caught the eye with some dazzling wing play in recent United–Birmingham encounters.

# 'Style and skill' versus 'kick-and-rush'

**Above right:** Wolves' England defenders Billy Wright and Bill Shorthouse join forces to shut out Tommy Taylor in a league clash at Old Trafford, 8 October 1955. They couldn't manage it for 90 minutes, however, Taylor scoring twice in a 4–3 victory. United and Wolves were undoubtedly the two teams of the decade, with three league titles apiece, though the footballing philosophies of their managers were poles apart. Wolves' boss Stan Cullis eschewed elaborate play in favour of a direct approach, which won more games than friends. It was denigrated by some as 'kick and rush' football, the antithesis of how Busby thought the game should be played. The United way was to nurture natural talent, then allow the players the freedom to express themselves on the field. This approach was closer to the 'push and run' style of Arthur Rowe's Spurs side

that won the championship in 1950–51, which was no great surprise as Rowe and Busby had worked closely together running the Army side during the war years.
**Below:** A crestfallen Bert Williams fumbles a shot from Tommy Taylor and the ball ends up in the back of Wolves' net. United finished the season on 60 points, 11 clear of Blackpool and Wolves. It was the most emphatic title victory since the First Division was expanded to 22 clubs and a 42-match league programme after World War I.
**Above left:** Maine Road, 29 January 1955. Manchester City's Don Revie wheels away thinking he has headed home, but the ball strikes the post and Bill Foulkes is on hand to clear. City still ran out winners in this FA Cup Fourth Round tie, and also did the double over United in the league that season. Reds' fans had the bragging rights when it came to the final table – fifth to

City's seventh – and there was even better to come the following season as more of the Youth Team stars were drafted into the senior side.
**Below right:** Jackie Blanchflower, one of the first of the 'Busby Babes' to be promoted into the first team. He made a solitary appearance in the title-winning 1951–52 season and became a regular on the teamsheet two years later.

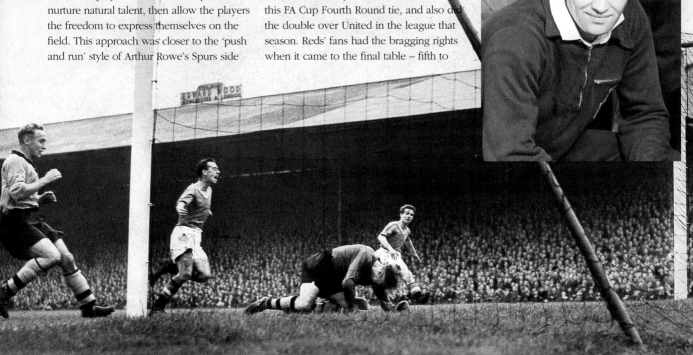

# Fortress Old Trafford paves way for title success

Bottom right: Tommy Taylor tries his hand at acrobatics, while Charlton's legendary 'keeper Sam Bartram strikes a ballet pose in a league match at the Valley, 26 December 1955. United went down 3–0, their worst defeat of the season coming a mere 24 hours after putting five goals past the same opposition at Old Trafford. It proved to be a blip in the team's upward fortunes, for United lost only once more in the league after the turn of the year. Home form was the key to United's fourth championship success: no team left Old Trafford with both points in 1955–56.

Top right: Roger Byrne pours the bubbly as Manchester United toast their second postwar championship. United finished 11 points clear of the pack, equalling Aston Villa's feat of 1896-97.

Middle: United take on Charlton in 1957.

Bottom left: Liam 'Billy' Whelan's mother flies in from Dublin with a cake to celebrate her son's 21st birthday on 1 April 1956. A gifted inside-forward, Whelan was a product of the same Home Farm club in Dublin where the young Johnny Carey made his first mark on the game.

---

**Home form was the key to United's fourth championship success: no team left Old Trafford with both points in 1955–56.**

---

# Busby vows to meet the European challenge

Middle right: Tommy Taylor and Roger Byrne celebrate United's 1955–56 championship with their girlfriends at a reception held at Manchester's Midland Hotel. United took the mantle from Chelsea, who had been 'advised' by the Football League not to enter that year's inaugural European Cup. Chelsea capitulated, but Busby resisted when the same pressures were brought to bear upon him. The United boss was far more perspicacious than the myopic administrators of the domestic game. 'Challenges should be met, not avoided,' he remarked, in typically ebullient fashion.

Bottom right: Having retained their league crown in 1956–57, United players turned their thoughts to celebrations of a domestic nature. Mark Jones, Tommy Taylor and Dennis Viollet look on as Jackie Blanchflower and new wife Jean cut the cake at their nuptials. Behind the newlyweds is Jackie's illustrious elder brother Danny, who would captain Spurs to the Double during United's post-Munich rebuilding period. Roger Byrne married fiancée Joy Cooper a few days later, and both couples honeymooned in Jersey, where they ran across Aston Villa's Peter McParland. The three players got on famously, indicating that there were no hard feelings over McParland's unsavoury contribution to the 1957 FA Cup final.

Top right: Roger Byrne leads United out for their first ever European Cup tie, at Anderlecht's Parc Astrid, 12 September 1956. Belgium's champions were completely overrun, United running out 12–0 aggregate winners. Busby said the 10–0 home win was 'as near perfect football as anyone could wish to see', while shell-shocked Anderlecht captain Jef Mermans wondered why the selectors didn't pick the entire side to represent England. Borussia Dortmund and Athletic Bilbao were also overcome, albeit not quite so easily. United had to overturn a

5–3 defeat in Spain, which they achieved with goals from Berry, Taylor and Viollet. All three 'home' games were staged at Maine Road, a throwback to the 1940s, but this time it was because Old Trafford lacked floodlights. These were installed in March 1957, in time for the semi-final encounter with Real Madrid. The holders proved too strong, winning 5–3 on aggregate, though Busby wasn't downhearted, for he knew his young side had gained valuable experience and was still improving, while di Stefano and Co. had an average age of 28. And having retained their league crown, United wouldn't have long to wait for another crack at the European Cup.

Bottom left: United winger David Pegg played his first international in February 1957. His debut was with the England Under-23s against Scotland Under-23s at Ibrox Park in Glasgow. He won his one and only senior cap in May of that year, in a 1-1 draw against the Republic of Ireland in Dublin.

# 'Smiling Assassin' not for sale

Top: A trademark towering header from Tommy Taylor piles on the agony for Arsenal at Old Trafford, 9 February 1957. United hit the Gunners for six in a 56-match season that saw the team rack up 142 goals. In only five outings did United draw a blank, and the man whose clinical finishing earned him the nickname the 'Smiling Assassin' once again led the way with 34 goals in 46 matches. At the end of the campaign Inter Milan tabled a massive £65,000 bid for Taylor but Busby wasn't about to part with his goal machine.

Middle right: Wilf McGuinness sporting a full head of hair as he makes his mark in the mid-1950s. It fell out almost overnight in the wake of his brief, stressful spell as manager in the late 1960s.

Middle left: Eddie Colman captained the side that won the Youth Cup in 1954–55, playing alongside Duncan Edwards in the half-back line. Edwards' power had already gained him promotion to the first team, but it was only a matter of time before the elegant Colman followed. His debut came in November 1955, and immediately the commentators were looking for superlatives to describe the mesmerising shimmy that earned him the nickname 'Snakehips'.

Bottom: Arsenal 'keeper Jack Kelsey deals with a United corner in a league clash at Highbury, 29 September 1956. Goals from Johnny Berry and Billy Whelan helped United to a 2–1 victory, giving United eight wins and two draws from their opening 10 games. The championship never looked in doubt, though the issue wasn't settled until title contenders Blackpool came to Old Trafford with three games to go. Needing a win to stay in the race, the Seasiders took the lead, but United hit back with late goals from Berry and Taylor. 28 wins and 64 points was the best return from a 42-match league programme since 1930–31, when Herbert Chapman's Arsenal lifted the title.

Inter Milan tabled a massive £65,000 bid for Taylor but Busby wasn't about to part with his goal machine.

# Murphy spurns top job offers

Top right: Fiery Welshman Jimmy Murphy was Matt Busby's right-hand man for 25 years, a key figure in the success United enjoyed in that time. Indeed, Bobby Charlton once said: 'I owe more to Jimmy Murphy than any other single person in football.' Murphy and Busby had crossed swords in their playing days – both were inside-forwards who had converted to outstanding half-backs, and each captained his country. Murphy was a hard taskmaster, instilling toughness in the players. His volatility complemented perfectly the mellower, more cerebral approach of his boss. Over the years several clubs tried to lure Murphy away with offers of a top job. Juventus came calling, and there was also an offer from Brazil, but Murphy preferred to remain as Number Two at Old Trafford. The exception was the job of Wales manager, which Murphy was able to do on a part-time basis. He was on international duty when the team travelled to Belgrade to play Red Star in February 1958. Coach Bert Whalley, who went in his stead, was one of the three non-playing United staff members to lose his life at Munich.

# Treble within sight for Babes

Above: Dean Court, 2 March 1957. Roger Byrne hooks the ball clear but only after a header from Bournemouth's Brian Bedford had crossed the line. The Third Division (South) side acquitted themselves well in this FA Cup quarter-final tie, but United came through 2–1, both goals coming from Johnny Berry. Berry also netted against his former club Birmingham City in the semis as United marched on to a Wembley meeting with Aston Villa and a possible Treble.
Middle left: Wilf McGuinness in training.
Below left: Roger Byrne studying for his physiotherapy exam with fiancée Joy, whom he met during the course. Byrne was a gifted all-round athlete but was already planning for a life after professional sport.
Far left: David Pegg pictured in 1957. Off the pitch he and Eddie Colman competed for the title of snappiest dresser around town.

The incident which almost certainly prevented United from becoming the first twentieth-century side to do the Double. With the 1957 FA Cup Final just six minutes old, Ray Wood was barged by Aston Villa's Peter McParland when the United 'keeper had the ball safely in hand. In the modern era the Irish winger would almost certainly have been shown a card of some hue, and even in the days when goalkeepers were afforded much less protection, the fact that McParland escaped censure was bewildering. Wood sustained a fractured cheekbone, and although he bravely returned to the fray just before

the half-hour mark, it was merely to provide nuisance value on the wing. Jackie Blanchflower took over between the sticks and performed heroically, but United did concede twice, both goals scored by the man who was lucky to be on the field. Fortune also favoured Villa for the second goal, as McParland looked to be in an offside position when Myerscough struck the woodwork, the Villa winger netting from the rebound. Well though United adapted, the team's rhythm was badly affected. Edwards had taken Blanchflower's centre-half berth, while withdrawing Whelan into the left-half

role vacated by Big Duncan meant that the attack was missing its top scorer that term. It was only after Tommy Taylor reduced United's arrears to 2–1 that a groggy Wood went back in goal and the original line-up was restored, but there were less than ten minutes to go and Villa ran the clock down to claim a seventh FA Cup victory. The Midlands club had also protected its record as the last to do the Double, back in 1896–97, though it had done so in circumstances that left a sour taste in the mouth. As one journalist commented: 'McParland was the man of the match – bagging two goals and one goalkeeper.'

Jackie Blanchflower kept Villa at bay for an hour after taking over from Ray Wood between the sticks before being beaten twice in the space of five minutes. Here, the 'Villan' of the piece Peter McParland fires Villa into the lead. His outrageous challenge on Ray Wood may have gone unpunished on the day, but it did add weight to the argument of those calling for the introduction of substitutes. Even so, the conservative nature of the footballing authorities meant that it would be almost a decade before the No.12 shirt became a regular sight on the field. The Football League allowed teams to replace an injured player in 1965–66, winger Willie Anderson taking the honour of becoming United's first substitute in that season's Charity Shield curtain-raiser against Liverpool. He came on for George Best in a game which ended in a 2–2 draw. This system lasted but a single year. It quickly became clear that injury could be feigned, so from 1966–67 tactical substitutions were permitted.

# Double chance evaporates

Tommy Taylor beats Aston Villa 'keeper Sims with a powerful header from a Duncan Edwards corner. It reduced United's arrears to 2–1 with seven minutes of the 1957 Cup Final to go. Busby put a dazed Ray Wood back in goal, allowing Jackie Blanchflower to return to the half-back line and Liam Whelan to push forward and boost the attack. Villa managed to hold out, preventing United from becoming the first twentieth century side to complete the Double. This was a period in which the FA Cup finals were blighted by serious injuries.

# Edwards lines up with England legends

Right: Duncan Edwards (centre) on international duty with England legends Stanley Matthews and Billy Wright. The trio were warming up for the Hampden Park clash with Scotland on 14 April 1956 in the Home International championship. Edwards was winning his fifth cap, while Matthews and Wright between them had made well over 100 appearances for their country. Even so, Edwards had already established himself as a star in Walter Winterbottom's side, a player who would undoubtedly have been a mainstay of the England team well into the 1960s had he survived Munich. The publishers evidently thought so, for Edwards had signed a book deal for penning his autobiography, Tackle Soccer This Way. The cover shot featured the Matthews–Edwards–Wright triumvirate, taken at this same Highbury training session. The book was published posthumously, with the family's blessing.

Below right and left: Ray Wood may be best remembered for battling bravely on after sustaining a broken cheekbone in the 1957 FA Cup Final, but he was a key member of the side that won back-to-back championships in 1955–56 and 1956–57.

Wood missed just four games in those two campaigns, an appearance record unmatched by any outfield player. He made his debut at 18, shortly after his arrival at Old Trafford in December 1949, but it wasn't until the 1953–54 season that he established himself as United's first choice 'keeper. New signing Harry Gregg displaced him during the 1957–58 season, for he never recaptured his best form after recovering from his Cup Final injury. Wood was on the plane for the fateful Red Star Belgrade trip, as cover for Gregg, and although he made a full recovery, he appeared just once more in a United shirt before being sold to Bill Shankly's Huddersfield Town.

**Asked why he had overlooked Edwards in his team talk. Jimmy Murphy shook his head ruefully. 'There is nothing to say that would help.'**

# 'Boom-Boom' brushes world champions aside

Above left: The keen-eyed United coaching staff studied all new young players, looking for any areas of their game that needed improvement. With Duncan Edwards they quickly discovered this was a fruitless exercise, such were his gifts in all facets of the game. Wearing his Wales manager's hat, Jimmy Murphy occasionally had the daunting task of having to prepare a team to face an England side that included Edwards. On one such occasion, having briefed his men about ten of the eleven opponents with whom they would be doing battle, he was asked why he had overlooked Edwards in his team talk. Murphy shook his head ruefully. 'There is nothing to say that would help.'

Above right: Duncan Edwards turning out for England against Scotland at Wembley, 6 April 1957. He notched his fourth international goal that day, the decisive strike in a 2–1 victory. A year earlier, Edwards' first international goal, against West Germany in Berlin, grabbed all the headlines. The reigning world champions had had England on the rack for the first quarter of the game, when 19-year-old Edwards launched a one-man assault on the opponents' goal, leaving defenders floundering in his wake before unleashing an unstoppable 25-yard piledriver. It turned the match in favour of England, who ran out 3–1 winners, while Edwards earned himself a new nickname: 'Boom-Boom'.

Below left: The elegant, gifted Liam 'Billy' Whelan top scored with 26 league goals in 1956–57, when United retained the championship. In an England– Eire match World Cup qualifier at Dalymount Park in May 1957 Whelan faced Duncan Edwards, one of four United team-mates in the England side that day. He nutmegged Edwards twice, something very few players managed to do. For all his talents Whelan was wracked by self-doubt and insecurity. On one occasion he asked Busby to leave him out of the side as he was out of form, short on confidence and struggling to contend with the barracking from the terraces. Busby replied: 'Worry when I have a go at you, son.'

# 'Snakehips': the babe of the Babes

Top right: What little footage survives from the 'Babes' era tends to focus on goalmouth action. Half-backs such as Eddie Colman live on in still photographs, and the memories of those who saw them play. The dapper, fashion-conscious Colman was as stylish on the pitch as off it. He made his debut just after his 19th birthday, in November 1955, having captained the side that completed a hat-trick of Youth Cup victories. Nicknamed 'Snakehips' for the trademark shimmy and jinking runs that mesmerized opponents, the diminutive Colman had a deft touch and slide-rule passing ability that perfectly complemented the powerhouse play of his half-back partner, Duncan Edwards. Had he not lost his life at Munich – the youngest of the Babes to be killed – 21-year-old Colman would surely have joined Edwards in the England side, and as he was also an aggressive tackler, he might have threatened the World Cup '66 place of another United legend, Nobby Stiles. Top left: Bill Foulkes; middle right: Roger Byrne; middle left: Johnny Berry. Bottom left and right: Wilf McGuinness may not have been the most gifted of the Busby Babes, but he accumulated an impressive cv before a broken leg cut short his career at the age of 22. McGuinness captained England Schoolboys and was a member of the famous Youth Cup-winning side before being drafted into the first-team in October 1955. He was primarily used as cover for Duncan Edwards, and many of his pre-Munich appearances came as a result of the versatile Edwards' being slotted into defence or the forward line to plug a gap. Injury caused McGuinness to miss the trip that ended in disaster on a Munich runway; his replacement in the squad, Geoff Bent, was among the eight fatalities on the playing staff. He took over the No. 6 shirt after the tragedy, and was a fixture in the side for almost two seasons, earning two England caps, before sustaining his career-ending injury. Busby signed Maurice Setters from West Bromwich Albion in January 1960 when it became clear that McGuinness would not make a full recovery.

# 'I have never seen a better left back'

Top and middle right: Matt Busby described Roger Byrne as an 'aristocratic' footballer. Lightning quick with balletic style, Byrne's defending was based on speed and impeccable positional play rather than rugged tackling. The Babes' captain regularly crossed swords with two of the greatest wingers of all time – Stanley Matthews and Tom Finney – and regularly got the better of them. Team-mate John Doherty said of his captain: 'He couldn't tackle, had no left foot – even though he played left full-back – was a poor header of the ball, and I have never seen a better left back in my life.'

Middle: Jackie Blanchflower made his debut as an 18-year-old in a goalless draw at Anfield on 24 November 1951, the same match in which Roger Byrne was promoted to the senior side. Reporting on their impressive first outings in the Manchester Evening News, journalist Tom Jackson headed his piece 'United's 'Babes' Cool, Confident'. It wasn't until the youngsters displaced the ageing members of the 1951–52 title-winning side that the term 'Busby Babes' became common currency. It was a neat media tag, though the manager himself is said to have hated the phrase.

Bottom left: Dennis Viollet made his debut as a 19-year-old in 1953, and over the next 10 years established himself as one of the greatest poachers in English football. He formed a deadly strike partnership with Tommy Taylor, the duo spearheading the championship successes of 1955–56 and 1956–57. In all competitions Viollet and Taylor between them hit the net 104 times in those two campaigns.

Bottom right: Dennis Viollet and wife Barbara, pictured at their Manchester home in September 1957.

# 'Wor Jackie' advises Bobby not to join Magpies

Right: Six United players were in Walter Winterbottom's 30-man England squad in 1956-57. Bobby Charlton turned 19 midway through that season and it was clearly only a matter of time before he joined Wood, Byrne, Taylor, Edwards, Berry and Pegg on international duty.

Below middle: Bobby Charlton and Matt Busby flanking a star-struck young Reds fan. Numerous clubs tracked the young Charlton, who stood out like a beacon in the junior teams he played for in and around Ashington. Newcastle United ought to have been favourite to gain his signature, but although he stood on the St James' Park terraces, he was a football rather than a Magpies fan. Moreover, his illustrious relative, Tyneside legend Jackie Milburn, specifically advised him against joining Newcastle as he felt it was a poorly run club which offered its young recruits little in the way of coaching.

Below left: Billy Whelan hit 33 goals in all competitions in 1956-57, his first full season in league football. Overall, Tommy Taylor edged him by one in the season's hotshot stakes, though the Irishman took top honours in the league with a 26-goal haul. In the early part of that championship-

Numerous clubs tracked the young Charlton, who stood out like a beacon in the junior teams he played for.

winning campaign Whelan scored in eight successive league games, a record which stood until the 2001–02 season, when Ruud van Nistelrooy went one better. Bobby Charlton took Whelan's place in the side midway through the 1957–58 season, though the latter was also in the squad that travelled to Belgrade for the ill-fated European Cup tie with Red Star. When someone uttered that they were going to die as the BEA Elizabethan attempted to take off for the third time, Whelan, a devout

Catholic, remarked: 'Well, I'm ready.'

Below right: Byrne was something of a firebrand in his younger days, his mood not helped by Busby's initial decision to play him on the wing, a position he disliked. After switching to full back he developed into one of the game's great defenders, and also matured into an outstanding leader. Many thought Busby was grooming his captain for a backroom role, or even the manager's hotseat.

Opposite below left: United take on Arsenal at Highbury on 1 February 1958, their last match on English soil. Edwards, Charlton and Taylor put United 3-0 up before half time but Arsenal bounced back, scoring three in three minutes. Viollet and Taylor put United 5-3 ahead in the second half and Tapscott's goal made the final score 4-5.

Opposite above: Duncan Edwards signs an autograph for a young fan on the pitch just before the kick-off.

Above:  Matt Busby pictured with some of his players at a training session in 1957. Left to right: Dennis Viollet, Tommy Taylor, David Pegg, Tom Curry (trainer), Wilf McGuinness, Roger Byrne, Matt Busby, Ray Wood, Bill Whelan, Duncan Edwards, Mark Jones, Geoff Bent and John Berry.

Right: Players at their lodgings at Ravenhurst Drive, near Old Trafford in 1957. Landlady Mrs Watson is on the left, and from her left, clockwise, Bobby Charlton, Billy Whelan, Jackie Blanchflower, Mark Jones, Gordon Clayton and Duncan Edwards.

Opposite below right: Mark Jones in action.

# Charlton first to get the Charlton treatment

Top right: Off the field Bobby Charlton was reserved and self-effacing; on it he had unswerving faith in his ability. United chief scout Joe Armstrong came to watch the 15-year-old prodigy in February 1953, having been tipped off by Charlton's primary school headmaster that here was a boy of rare talent. Armstrong, the man responsible for bringing a number of the 'Babes' to the club, knew immediately that he was looking at a future star. Busby endorsed that view when he watched Bobby play for England schoolboys, and

moved quickly to secure his signature ahead of the chasing pack of clubs. Charlton became a United player in June that year, though it would be three years before he made his first-team debut – against Charlton Athletic! Days before turning 19, Charlton celebrated his call-up by scoring two thunderbolts in a 4–2 win – despite carrying an ankle injury.

Top middle: Dennis Viollet returned to action for the last few games of the 1957–58 season, including the Cup Final, though it was clear that he was far from fully fit. The man who missed out was Shay Brennan, who had scored three goals in the competition, including one in the semi-final victory over Fulham.

Top left: The Blanchflower brothers prepare to face an England side including three United players – Byrne, Edwards and Taylor – in a Home International match at Wembley, 6 November 1957. Jackie and Danny came out on top that day, Northern Ireland registering their

first victory over England for 30 years, and their first on English soil since 1914. Duncan Edwards scored his fifth and final goal for England in the 3–2 defeat. Taylor's last two international goals came three weeks later, in a 4–0 Wembley victory over France, the last game England played before the Munich disaster.

Bottom: Smiles all round as Busby and Murphy conclude the deal to take Harry Gregg from Doncaster Rovers to Old Trafford in December 1957. Rovers' manager was Northern Ireland legend Peter Doherty (second left), idol to all aspiring young footballers in Ulster in the 1930s and 40s, including Gregg, Billy Whelan and Jackie Blanchflower. Belle Vue secretary Bill Dickinson (left) looks well pleased at having secured a record £23,000 deal for a goalkeeper. It didn't look such a good piece of business six months later, when Rovers finished bottom of Division Two.

Below right: Roger Byrne with fiancée Joy Cooper.

# Supremacy on a shoestring

Above: Of the team which won consecutive league titles in 1955–56 and 1956–67, only Ray Wood, Tommy Taylor and Johnny Berry joined the club for fee, a combined total of £50,000. The eight other 'core' players in those glorious two campaigns were: Foulkes, Byrne, Colman, Jones, Edwards, Whelan, Viollet and Pegg. If that wasn't testimony enough to Busby's managerial skills and the endeavour of the United scouts, nine other squad players who contributed to those two championship successes were also zero-fee acquisitions: Ian Greaves, Geoff Bent, Jeff Whitefoot, Jackie Blanchflower, Colin Webster, Albert Scanlon, Freddie Goodwin, Wilf McGuinness and Bobby Charlton. The white-coated duo, Bill Inglis (left) and Tom Curry, were responsible for the development of many young players after

they joined the training staff in the mid-1930s. Inglis had been a fringe player at United in the 20s, while Curry had enjoyed a much more successful playing career with Newcastle United. Both had a genial disposition which was the perfect foil for the volatile Jimmy Murphy, whose fiery temperament kept the youngsters on their mettle. Curry was killed in the Munich crash, along with coach Bert Whalley. The loss of two key members of the backroom team received fewer headlines than the deaths of eight star players, but insiders recognised it as a severe blow to the smooth running of the club.

Right: Club captain Roger Berry lifted the championship trophy in 1955-56 and again the following year. When United retained their title in 1956-57, Busby's 11-year League record read: 2-2-2-4-2-1-8-4-5-1-1.

# Champagne form brings Babes a second league title

Top: Cracking open the bubbly in the communal bath after securing back-to-back championships in 1956–57. In a season of extraordinary consistency, United recorded identical home and away records. If 14 wins, four draws and three defeats showed solid home form, the same statistics on the road was hugely impressive. Neither was there much between the side's home and away record in terms of the goals column: 48 away goals – over two per game on average – was only seven fewer than the team scored at Old Trafford. The defence shipped 25 goals at home, and only four more than that on their travels. Ironically, the largest blip in an otherwise magnificent campaign occurred on 20 October 1956, when Everton came to Old Trafford and scored a 5–2 win. The Reds got their revenge in the return fixture at Goodison Park in March, by which time they were well on their way to taking the league crown for the fifth time in the club's history.
Middle left: Ronnie Cope in 1958, the year he scored his two goals for the senior side. Cope made 100 appearances in the United first team between 1956 and 1961.
Middle right: Bill Foulkes began as full back but would take over as the immoveable object at the heart of the defence, in the mould of Allenby Chilton. Both were teak-tough ex-miners, uncompromising players who were as vital to the side as the graceful artists. Both had brief international careers: Chilton was called up twice to the England

side, while Foulkes joined the ranks of the one-cap wonders in October 1954, in a 2–0 away win over Northern Ireland.
Bottom right: Matt Busby's aunt, Delia O'Donnell, was the surprise guest when her nephew featured on This Is Your Life in January 1958. As a player and manager Busby had already achieved more than enough to merit being the subject of the prestigious TV show, though many more triumphs lay ahead. Ironically, Busby faced an immediate headache of trying to keep a reserve side packed with internationals happy. Ray Wood, who had just lost his place in the side to Harry Gregg, had put in a transfer request, while Johnny Berry, no longer an automatic choice, was also in talks over his position. A month later, the situation would be very different. Far from intense competition for places, the Munich disaster would leave Jimmy Murphy scratching around trying to field a team.

PART TWO

The Undefeated

# 'I knew we were going to crash'

A poignant shot of Kenny Morgans and Tommy Taylor souvenir hunting in Munich, during the stop-over on the outward journey to Belgrade. Taylor was among the victims, while Morgans, who had just broken into the side, was never the same player after the accident and soon moved on to Swansea.

The Babes listen attentively to what would be their last ever team talk. Matt Busby impresses on his players what will be required for United to go through against Red Star Belgrade in the 1957-58 European Cup quarter-final. They undoubtedly took heed, turning a narrow 2-1 advantage gained at Old Trafford into a seemingly unassailable 5-1 lead with a scintillating first-half display in Belgrade. It

was enough, though only just, as Red Star struck three times after the break. The early editions of the Manchester Evening News exulted over the team's display; 24 hours later, the score barely warranted a footnote.

The fateful tyre marks left by the aircraft in the snow.

The wreckage of the BEA Elizabethan aircraft lies strewn across the runway at Munich airport. The accident claimed 23 lives, including those of eight United players.

> 'It seems a funny thing to say but I knew we were going to crash as we made that third fatal trip up the runway. I felt dreadful. We had failed to get off twice and none of us wanted to go back in the plane. We had had enough.' HARRY GREGG

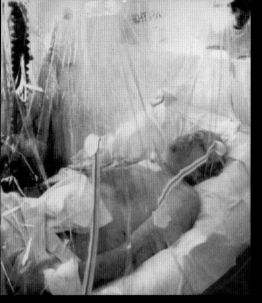

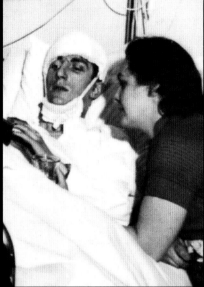

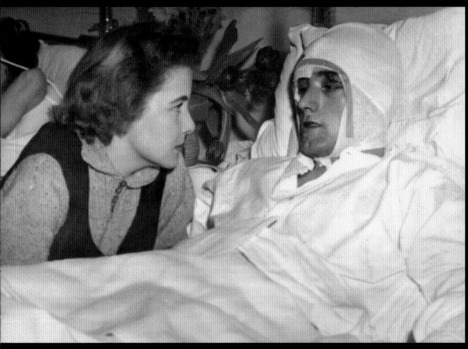

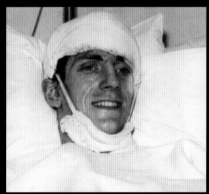

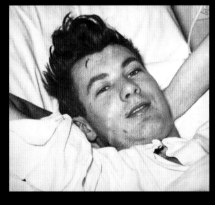

# Pegg move sealed his fate

**Top left:** Matt Busby lies in an oxygen tent, hovering between life and death. He suffered multiple injuries, including a shattered foot which had to be reset without anaesthetic because of a punctured lung. Busby's personal road to recovery was a long and painful one, yet the physical wounds were as nothing compared with the emotional scars Munich left. Busby said that one of the lowest points was when Johnny Berry, who was himself grievously injured, came to Busby's room and bemoaned the fact that Tommy Taylor hadn't bothered to pay him a visit. Taylor had died instantly in the crash.

**Top right and centre [illegible]:** Dennis Viollet manages a smile and enjoys a visit from wife Barbara as he recovers from his injuries, which were relatively minor. Known by his team-mates as 'Tricky' for his speed and cunning in and around the box, Viollet lived up to his nickname by breaking Jack Rowley's goalscoring record in 1959–60.

**Middle [illegible]:** Josephine Scanlon pays a bedside visit to check on her husband's progress. Albert Scanlon was among the lucky ones who not only survived the crash but recovered to play first-team football again. He had been playing cards with Bill Foulkes, Kenny Morgans and David Pegg, the four of them seated towards the front of the plane. Before the third fateful take-off attempt, an apprehensive Pegg moved to the rear, believing it to be a safer position. He was killed, while the three other card school members all survived.

**Below left and right:** Flying winger Kenny Morgans made his senior team debut barely six weeks before Munich, taking Johnny Berry's outside-right berth. Eighteen-year-old Morgans played in both European Cup quarter-final matches against Red Star Belgrade, and recovered in time to line up against AC Milan in the semis. Gregg, Foulkes, and Viollet were the only other players to feature in both ties. Bobby Charlton was also back playing, but he was required for England duty. The club versus country debate has long been a bone of contention, but in 1958 the pecking order was crystal clear: pre-World Cup friendlies against Portugal and Yugoslavia took precedence over United's bid to reach the European Cup final. It must have left a bitter taste in the mouths of Reds' fans when Charlton was discarded for the tournament the following month.

# 'I am not God'

**Above left:** Bill Foulkes and Harry Gregg survived the Munich crash virtually unscathed, though the loss of eight team-mates and three of their mentors on the United staff must have taken a heavy toll on their psychological well-being. On their overland trip home the two insisted on the train window remaining open as they experienced understandable feelings of claustrophobia. Even so, Gregg and Foulkes took the field for United's Cup tie against Sheffield Wednesday 13 days after the accident. Kenny Morgans, Bobby Charlton and Dennis Viollet all saw first-team action before the season was out, while Albert Scanlon returned in time for the start of the 1958-59 campaign. It was a period of grieving for those lost while at the same time looking to the future. As an example of the need for continuity, Foulkes, the new club captain, took over Roger Byrne's regular column in the *Manchester Evening News*.

---

### Gregg and Foulkes took the field for United's Cup tie against Sheffield Wednesday 13 days after the accident.

---

**Middle left:** Fans line the road as a hearse carrying a victim of the Munich air disaster drives past in Manchester.
**Middle right:** Johnny Berry's wife on her way to visit her husband in hospital. Berry sustained such serious head injuries that Harry Gregg recognized him as one of the players only through the club blazer he was wearing. He remained in a coma for two months and, like his manager, was given last rites. When surgeon Georg Maurer accompanied Jimmy Murphy round the ward giving his prognosis on each of the United players, he shrugged when they came to Berry's bed and said: 'I am not God.' Berry must have had a constitution that belied his waif-like frame, for he did recover and was to live for another 36 years, though, inevitably, his days as a professional footballer were at an end.
**Below:** The surviving air crew of the British Airways European Airways Flight 609. (l-r) James Thain, Rosemary Cheverton, Margaret Bellis and George Rodgers.

# Domestic authorities block UEFA gesture

Below: Spurs and Manchester City players stand in silence as a mark of respect to those who lost their lives in the Munich tragedy. United, who had been on course for a hat-trick of league titles, were in the semi-final of the European Cup and the Fifth Round of the FA Cup. Eight players lost their lives, while Johnny Berry and Jackie Blanchflower never played again. Incredibly, Harry Gregg and Bill Foulkes took the field for the Cup clash with

Sheffield Wednesday on 19 February, just 13 days after the accident. Jimmy Murphy's side, comprising reserves, Youth Team players and emergency signings, won 3–0, Shay Brennan scoring twice on his debut. The goodwill shown by the FA in allowing United to field the 'ineligible' Stan Crowther dissipated at the end of the season, when the club was offered an ex gratia place in the 1958–59 European Cup draw, along with champions Wolves. It

was a magnanimous gesture on the part of Uefa towards a club that had finished ninth in the league, but the domestic footballing authorities, who had been dragged kicking and screaming into accepting a Europe-wide competition, refused consent. United would have faced Young Boys Berne, who went on to reach the semis; thus, even the depleted 1958–59 side might have gone all the way, nine years before Bobby Charlton lifted the trophy.

# A tie for a tourniquet, a coal lorry for an ambulance

**Below left:** Dennis Viollet recuperating at home with his family, March 1958.

**Below right:** Jackie Blanchflower leaves Rechts Der Isar hospital with wife Jan on 13 March 1958. Blanchflower suffered kidney and liver damage that would cause him health problems for the rest of his life. When Harry Gregg found him in the wreckage, the goalkeeper's more immediate concern was Blanchflower's right arm, which had been virtually severed in the crash. Gregg, who had played in the same Northern Ireland boys' team as Blanchflower, used his tie as a tourniquet to stem the blood loss before a coal lorry, the first vehicle on the scene, was able to transport them and the other injury victims to hospital.

**Right:** Thousands of Dubliners line the route taken by the funeral cortege as Billy Whelan is laid to rest at Glasnevin Cemetery. Whelan had suffered a loss of form and lost his place in the team to Bobby Charlton just before Christmas 1957. He had asked to be excused from the Belgrade trip, but Busby was insistent that he remain part of the squad.

**Bottom:** The Dean of Manchester, the Very Reverend H A Jones, leads a service prior to United's game against Nottingham Forest on 22 February, the first league match since the accident. The game ended in a 1–1 draw. United saved their best form for the FA Cup, and were swept to Wembley on a tide of emotion. In the immediate aftermath of Munich the weekly grind of league football was beyond the limits of the team cobbled together by Jimmy Murphy.

> Billy Whelan had asked to be excused from the Belgrade trip, but Busby was insistent that he remain part of the squad.

# 'Keep the flag flying'

Bill Inglis leads a training session at White City days after the Munich crash. A lot of responsibility fell on Inglis's shoulders as Jimmy Murphy had more than a savagely depleted team to contemplate. He oversaw the repatriation of the bodies, which were housed initially in the Old Trafford gymnasium, and liaised with the families of the bereaved regarding funeral arrangements. Harry Gregg recalled stealing upon the desolate figure of Murphy shortly after the crash to find him venting his anguish in a flood of tears. The Welshman turned to alcohol to numb the pain. He did what Busby had asked of him – 'keep the flag flying until I get back' – but discharging his duty came at a high price.

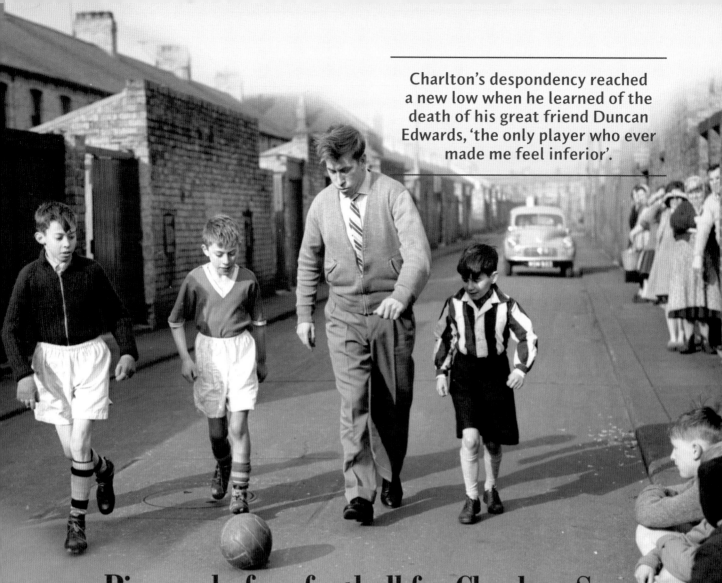

# Pigeons before football for Charlton Snr

Left: The indefatigable Elizabeth 'Cissie' Charlton, pictured with the more famous of her sons outside the family's Ashington home. Bobby's father was a coalminer, yet the Charltons didn't conform to the working-class stereotype for menfolk in north-east mining towns in the 1950s: that the pit and football dominated their lives. Bob Snr preferred pigeons to the round-ball game. When Bobby scored twice against Portugal in the 1966 World Cup semi-final – widely regarded as his finest hour in an England jersey – his father was neither at Wembley nor glued to the television, choosing instead to work his usual underground shift. Cissie's love of the game, by contrast, was genetically imprinted. Generations of Milburns – her family name – had turned out for good amateur sides, while all four of her brothers played League football. The most famous member of the Milburn clan was cousin Jackie, the Newcastle and England legend. Above: The golden boy of English football's most glamorous club side returns to his roots and indulges in a kickabout with a gaggle of star-struck local youngsters. It was an unmissable photo-opportunity for the Press, though it didn't quite tell the whole story.

Bobby Charlton had suffered only minor head wounds at Munich but was sent home to recover from the mental scarring the crash had left. Inevitably, reporters laid siege to the family home in Beatrice Street, and it was Cissie who persuaded her reluctant son to pose for the cameras. The tone of the reportage was optimistic, yet Charlton became deeply depressed, even contemplating ending his footballing career. His despondency reached a new low when he learned of the death of his great friend Duncan Edwards, 'the only player who ever made me feel inferior'. All thoughts of quitting the game soon evaporated, though the tragedy had a lasting effect on his personality. Never the most outgoing of people, Charlton became noticeably more serious and insular. It was as if jocularity might be construed as a betrayal of the friends he had lost in the crash. When Sandy Busby picked out a fashionable Italian-styled coat for Bobby to wear on the journey home from Munich, the latter condemned it as 'too flash'. From now on, Charlton would save the exuberant showmanship for the football pitch.

# 'Manchester United will rise again'

Right: 18 April 1958. Well-wishers turn out in force as Matt Busby returns to Manchester. It was 71 days before he was well enough to leave Rechts der Isar Hospital, during which time he had twice received last rites. In his absence it was left to Jimmy Murphy to pick up the pieces. Murphy had missed the ill-fated trip because of his managerial commitments to the Welsh national side. Wales had been eliminated from the 1958 World Cup but had been thrown a lifeline by Fifa, who drew lots to decide which country would face Israel, then a pariah state in international football. Wales came out of the hat, and thus a lottery may well have saved Murphy's life. Not only that, but Wales went on to defeat Israel in the play-off and claim a place in the World Cup finals in Sweden, where they performed heroically before going down to eventual winners Brazil in the quarter-finals.
Top and below: March 1958. Manchester rolls out the red carpet for Professor Georg

Maurer and his wife Erika (2nd and 3rd left), along with members of the medical team that treated the Munich survivors. Club Chairman Harold Hardman had paid tribute to Professor Maurer and his team in United Review,19 February 1958. The piece was laden with sadness, though the tone was defiantly optimistic:

'Although we mourn our dead and grieve for our wounded we believe that great days are not done for us. The sympathy and encouragement of the football world and particularly of our supporters will justify and inspire us. The road back may be long and hard but with the memory of those who died at Munich, of their stirring achievements and wonderful sportsmanship ever with us, Manchester United will rise again.'

The programme was printed with a blank teamsheet as it was unclear right up to the last hour who would be available to face Sheffield Wednesday in the Fifth Round FA Cup tie.

# Manchester honours Munich medical team

**Below right:** Chairman Harold Hardman accompanies Professor Maurer onto the pitch before United's home game against West Bromwich Albion, 8 March 1958. A recorded message by Matt Busby was played over the tannoy to provide a further fillip for the team and supporters.

**Below left:** Bill Foulkes, Dennis Viollet and Harry Gregg in conversation with two of the doctors from Professor Maurer's medical team.

**Bottom left and right:** Bill Foulkes presents Frau Maurer with a bouquet, the surgeon's wife responding by pinning a flower on Harry Gregg's shirt as a good luck token before the West Brom game. It didn't have the desired effect on the outcome, for Gregg had to pick the ball out of the net four times, without reply from United. The events of 6 February rendered results of secondary importance, and Gregg's place in the club's affections was secure irrespective of his form between the sticks. Ignoring the threat that the plane might explode, Gregg pulled

Bobby Charlton and Dennis Viollet clear of the wreckage, tended to Jackie Blanchflower and rescued two other passengers, Vera Lukic and her 22-month-old daughter Vesna.

**Above right:** Kenny Morgans and his 18-year-old fiancée Stephanie Lloyd arrive back in Manchester on 6 March, one month after the crash. Dennis Viollet returned home at the same time, both men taking an overland route.

**Middle right:** Jimmy Murphy looks on as Blackpool inside-forward Ernie Taylor signs on the dotted line.

**Bottom right:** Matt Busby's reading matter says it all. After Munich there was, almost inevitably, a low period when Busby doubted his will to rebuild the United team yet again. The indomitable spirit soon surfaced, and Busby was in his usual place in the dug-out when United met Bolton in the FA Cup Final, less than three months after the crash, though Jimmy Murphy led the team onto the Wembley turf.

# Championship contenders against the odds

Above right: Bobby Charlton became Matt Busby's most important lieutenant after Munich. Of the Babes who survived the accident, Charlton best represented the youthful flair and élan of the championship-winning side of 1956 and 1957. The 20-year-old rose to the challenge, his teammates noticing that he suddenly developed a maturity beyond his years. Charlton returned to first-team action on 1 March and won his first England cap six weeks later, scoring in a 4–0 win over Scotland at Hampden Park on 19 April.

Middle right: Old Trafford, 5 April 1958. Right-half Freddie Goodwin in action against Preston North End, a game that ended in a goalless draw. Goodwin had made only sporadic first-team appearances since turning professional with United in October 1953, finding himself behind Don Gibson – Busby's son-in-law through marriage to his daughter Sheena – and Jeff Whitefoot in the pecking order. Goodwin's chances diminished still further once the Colman–Edwards partnership took root midway through the 1955–56 season, but he was ever-present in 1958–59, making an important contribution as United exceeded all expectations by vying for the championship with Wolves.

Below right: Physiotherapist Ted Dalton checks out the 32-year-old legs of new recruit Ernie Taylor. He made just 30 appearances for United but his vast experience and ability to put his foot on the ball was vital at a time when a host of second-string players were thrown into first-team action. With his neat flicks and clever backheels, Taylor also played his part in ensuring that entertainment remained firmly on the agenda during the rebuilding process.

Bottom: Highbury, 26 March 1958. Alex Dawson opens in the scoring in the FA cup semi-final replay against Fulham. The Black Prince, as he was known, went on to complete a hat-trick, a month after turning 18. United won the match 5–3.

Below left: Jimmy Murphy puts his point across to Bobby Charlton and new signing Ernie Taylor as United battle on manfully after Munich. Murphy contemplated a bold move to sign Puskas from Real Madrid, but decided it was against the spirit of a club that had established a reputation for bringing youngsters through the ranks. Reinforcements were needed, however, and the diminutive Taylor – nicknamed Tom Thumb – was bought as a stopgap, to add experience to the depleted team. He was on United's books for less than a year, but in that time the effervescent 32-year-old gave enormous help to youngsters such as Kenny Morgans, Alex Dawson, Mark Pearson and Shay Brennan, who suddenly found themselves catapulted into the spotlight. Taylor was a two-time FA Cup winner, with Newcastle United in 1951 and Blackpool two years later – the 'Matthews Final'. He was also a one-cap wonder for England, though he chose his game badly: his sole appearance came in the famous 6–3 defeat by the Puskas's Magyars in 1953.

# Unsung heroes

Four players who made an important, if limited, contribution to United's cause in the 1950s. Defenders Ian Greaves (bottom right) and Ronnie Cope (middle right and bottom left) were on the club's books for 17 years between them, yet their aggregate appearance record was fewer than 200 games. Ronnie Cope, a former schoolboy international, began 1958 as an understudy to Mark Jones and Jackie Blanchflower, and those two players looked set to keep him in the Reserve team for some time to come. Cope admirably filled the void left by Mark Jones after Munich until Bill Foulkes switched from full-back to centre-half during the 1960–61 season, at the end of which Cope joined Luton Town. As a centre-forward Alex Dawson (pictured this page, top right, with Ernie Taylor) had even bigger boots to fill. A prolific striker at every level, Dawson hit 54 goals in his 93 appearances in a United shirt, but never managed to reach the heights of the great Tommy Taylor. He was just 21 when he was sold to Preston in October 1961, by which time David Herd had arrived from Arsenal to stake first claim on the No.9 jersey.

**Top left**: Bill Foulkes captained the side after Munich, a responsibility that did not sit easily with him in the wake of the tragedy; it wasn't long before he asked Busby to relieve him of the duty. He still had more than a decade left in him as a player, though, and by the time he hung up his boots, Foulkes had overtaken the appearance record of the great Joe Spence, United's star striker of the interwar years. Only three men have since eclipsed Foulkes' record of 688 appearances in a United shirt: Bobby Charlton, Ryan Giggs and Paul Scholes, Giggs going on to pass the 900-game mark for the Reds.

**Middle left**: Commentator Kenneth Wolstenholme interviews Dennis Viollet before the 1958 FA Cup Final. Viollet had had a couple of league outings since Munich and was declared fit to join Harry Gregg, Bill Foulkes and Bobby Charlton in the team that took the field at Wembley on 3 May to face Bolton. Just before the crash Viollet had scored twice in a 7–2 mauling of Bolton at Old Trafford, and despite United's unsurprising slump in the run-in, the team still finished five points and six places above the men from Burnden Park.

# United swept to Wembley on tide of emotion

Above: The team that took the field against Bolton Wanderers in the Cup Final was unrecognizable as the one that started the 1957–58 season. Foulkes, Charlton and Viollet were there, while Harry Gregg had signed from Doncaster Rovers two months before the accident for a British record £23,000. The rest of the side had an unfamiliar look. Ronnie Cope, Freddie Goodwin, Alex Dawson, Ian Greaves and Colin Webster were all promoted from within. Ernie Taylor – a two-time Cup winner already with Blackpool and Newcastle – was signed from Blackpool as a stopgap. Wing-half Stan Crowther, who had played against United in the 1957 FA Cup Final, joined from Aston Villa barely an hour before United's postponed Fifth Round tie with Sheffield Wednesday on 19 February. He should have been Cup-tied, having already played for Villa in that season's competition, but with Villa already out of the competition United were given special dispensation from the FA to allow him to play. The new-look side had put out favourites West Bromwich Albion, and 18-year-old Alex Dawson had scored a hat-trick in the semi-final replay against Fulham. The whole country seemed to be willing United on to Cup glory, the second time in five years that Bolton had faced a tide of sentiment in the opposition's favour. In 1953 the country had its way and Blackpool's Stanley Matthews finally claimed his winners' medal. This time Bolton were determined to spoil the party.

Back row (l to r): Goodwin, Dawson, Cope, Gregg, Greaves, Crowther. Front row: Viollet, Taylor, Foulkes, Webster, Charlton.

Left: Freddie Goodwin was a stylish wing-half who chalked up most of his 107 appearances in the two years following the Munich crash. He signed for Leeds in March 1960, leaving one Charlton behind to join forces with another. Jackie's Leeds side had just been relegated, and would remain in Division Two until 1963-64, when they returned to the top flight in style as champions. Goodwin moved on and started to make his name in management, thereby missing out on some incendiary Roses battles. Leeds became one of United's fiercest rivals, finishing runners-up to Busby's men in their first season back in the top division.

# Baggies force replay

United face their stiffest test en route to Wembley in 1958, a Sixth Round FA Cup tie against a West Bromwich Albion side that had beaten the pre-Munich side 4–3 at the Hawthorns earlier in the season and would go on to finish fourth in Division One. This was the game when Bobby Charlton returned to action, though it was Ernie Taylor and Alex Dawson who were on target in a thrilling 2–2 draw.

**Above:** Dawson is pictured netting with his head after Taylor's 25-yard drive came back off the woodwork. With less than five minutes to go United were clinging to a 2–1 lead, but West Brom equalized.

**Below:** Despite Harry Gregg's desperate efforts, the ball is adjudged to have crossed the line in the dying minutes of the FA Cup Sixth Round clash at West Bromwich Albion, 1 March 1958. A 2–2 draw meant that the two teams locked horns again at Old Trafford four days later, a game that sent Reds' fans into a ferment. A 60,000 capacity crowd packed the ground long before kick-off, leaving an estimated 20,000 locked out and forced to make do with a radio commentary interspersed with live sound effects. The biggest roar of the night came when United's Colin Webster scored the only goal of the match to set up a semi-final meeting with Fulham. United must have given their all to the Cup cause that night, for when West Brom returned to Manchester three days later for a league match, the Midlands side ran out easy 4–0 winners.

**Left:** The camera doesn't lie. Ronnie Cope can't quite believe it but Daily Mail pictures confirm that he failed to clear the ball before it crossed the line at the Hawthorns, 1 March 1958. Albion's late goal levelled the scores and forced a replay at Old Trafford.

---

**With less than five minutes to go United were clinging to a 2–1 lead, but West Brom equalized to force a replay.**

---

# Emotional final a game too far

**Below:** Matt Busby and Jimmy Murphy look on anxiously as United struggle to get to grips with a dominant Bolton Wanderers side in the 1958 Cup Final. The Reds had hammered Bolton 7–2 in the league just before the trip to Belgrade, but they were a different proposition this time round, battle-hardened and determined to carry off the silverware. It proved to be a game too far for United, who fell to a Nat Lofthouse double, the killer second goal coming from a clattering challenge which saw both Gregg and ball bundled into the net. It was highly controversial even by the more liberal standards of the day, yet Busby and Gregg magnanimously conceded that no foul had been committed and the better team had won. In the 1920s Bolton had appeared in three Cup finals in the space of six years, using 17 players; United had deployed 20 men in successive appearances in the domestic showpiece. 'Emotion and spirit had kept us going for a long time,' said Bill Foulkes, 'but after a while it was not enough.' United became the first team to lose in successive Wembley finals, but the jerseys worn that day showed that resurrection was under way: they bore a phoenix motif.

**Above right:** Ernie Taylor lends a supportive hand to Bolton's Dennis Stevens

after the latter was knocked unconscious during the 1958 Cup Final. It was Stevens who came out on top, while Taylor picked up a losers' medal for the first time in three Wembley visits. What should have been the proudest day in Stevens' footballing career was marred by the fact that he was personally touched by the Munich tragedy. He and Duncan Edwards were second cousins, the two having played together for Dudley Schools before going on to fight many battles at professional level.

**Middle right:** Manchester United wives (and mother) on a day out in Bayswater. From left to right, Irene Cope, Winifred Greaves, Sylvia Goodwin, Mavis Gregg and Cissie Charlton, Bobby's mother.

United became the first team to lose in successive Wembley finals, but the jerseys worn that day showed that resurrection was under way: they bore a phoenix motif.

# Crompton returns to Old Trafford fold

**Above:** The United team in the immediate post-Munich period, which would have been unfamiliar to all but die-hard Reds' fans. Back row: Bobby Harrop, Ian Greaves, Freddie Goodwin, Harry Gregg, Stan Crowther, Ronnie Cope, Shay Brennan. Front row: Jack Crompton, Alex Dawson, Mark Pearson, Bill Foulkes, Ernie Taylor, Colin Webster, Bill Inglis. The effects of Munich weren't felt on the pitch alone. The loss of Tom Curry and Bert Whalley, along with the temporary elevation of Jimmy Murphy to the manager's hotseat, left trainer Bill Inglis with too much to do. Jack Crompton, United's stalwart 'keeper of the postwar years, answered the call, returning to the club two years after departing to join the backroom team at Luton Town. Of the young players who were thrust into the first-team spotlight, only Shay Brennan had a long-term impact. For England schoolboy international Alex Dawson the promotion probably came too quickly. Busby had given the promising centre-forward a couple of outings at the back end of the 1956–57 season – he scored on his league debut against Burnley – and was obviously nurturing his development. In the event, the highlight of his United career came at just 18 years 33 days, when he hit a hat-trick in the FA Cup semi-final replay against Fulham. He left to join Preston North End in 1961.

**Right above:** Dennis Viollet was something of a party animal before Munich and was even more determined to live life to the full after his brush with death. It was a lifestyle which didn't sit well with Busby and probably hastened Viollet's exit from Old Trafford in 1961, when he was still at the top of his game.

**Below right:** Busby signed utility forward Colin Webster on the recommendation of Dennis Viollet, who served with him in the army. Webster spent six years at Old Trafford, but although he went to the 1958 World Cup with Wales, he never commanded a regular first-team spot at United until the back end of the 1957-58 season. Having missed the fateful trip to Belgrade to play Red Star with a bout of 'flu, he had his best run in the side, the highlight of which was that year's Wembley final against Bolton. Webster was the hero of the hour when he scored the goal that beat favourites West Bromwich Albion in a quarter-final replay, providing the finish after a dazzling Bobby Charlton run. He left the club to join Swansea Town in October of that year.

# What price a United title hat-trick?

Left: White Hart Lane, 12 April 1958. Harry Gregg gathers under pressure from Spurs' centre-forward Bobby Smith, but he did have to pick the ball out of the back of the net once, United losing the match 1–0. Unsurprisingly, United's league form nose-dived after Munich, the scratch side put together by Jimmy Murphy winning just one of its last 14 Division One games. It was all very different on 1 February, when the Reds signed off on domestic soil by winning a nine-goal thriller at Highbury. United were then lying second to Wolves, handily placed to complete a hat-trick of championship successes. Even though the team showed relegation form after Munich, United still managed to finish in the top half of the table, 21 points behind the title-winning Midlands side. Wolves' record was almost identical to United's the previous year: Won 28, Drew 8, Lost 6, with 103 goals scored. The only difference was in the 'Goals Against' column. How many points the pre-Munich side would have garnered from those 28 up for grabs in the last three months of the season is a matter of speculation, but the title would certainly have been well within their compass.

Below right: Busby meets Joe Mercer, the new Aston Villa manager ahead of the two sides' tie at Old Trafford in December 1958. United proved too good for Villa and won the match 2-0 on Mercer's debut.

Below left and bottom: Manchester United's latest signing, Albert Quixall, in action.

# Busby back at the helm

Top: August 1958. Six months after the Munich air disaster Manchester United return to Germany to take part in a special thanksgiving match.

**Above:** 6 May 1958. Matt Busby shares a joke with the Mayor of Stretford, Edward Reid, at a Town Hall reception held in honour of the Manchester United manager and his team. The scenes that greeted the United team on its arrival back in Manchester could scarcely have been more chaotic had Bill Foulkes lifted the trophy at Wembley.

**Left:** After a six-month recuperation, Matt Busby was back at the helm at the start of the 1958–59 season. The manager hadn't dipped into the transfer market between 1953 and 1957, but the rebuilding process this time involved developing home-grown talent and wielding the chequebook. Busby's first major signing was Albert Quixall, bought to add punch to an attack shorn of Tommy Taylor's mighty contribution. Twenty-five-year-old Quixall was the golden boy of English football, a crowd-pleasing flair player who was a full international by the age of 20. He had impressed Jimmy Murphy when playing against United for Sheffield Wednesday in the emotional first post-Munich match at Old Trafford. Wednesday were a yo-yo club in the 1950s, and having just been relegated from the top flight yet again, the club was willing to part with its most valuable asset. Busby had to pay a British record £45,000 to get his man, but the need for a finished product was urgent.

**Below:** 26 April 1959. United depart for an end-of-season friendly in Holland, the first club-organized flight since the Munich disaster 14 months earlier. The first rebuilding season was remarkably successful, United racking up 103 goals in finishing runners-up to Wolves. Quixall made a quiet start, with just four goals, while fringe players such as Freddie Goodwin, Wilf McGuinness, Ian Greaves and Albert Scanlon became regular first teamers.

# Bernabeu extends hand of friendship

**Below:** Old Trafford, 2 October 1959. United on the receiving end of a six-goal drubbing at the hands of Real Madrid, including two goals each from di Stefano and Puskas. This was no European Cup debacle, but a testament to the mutual respect that existed between the two pre-eminent club sides on the Continent. The Spanish giants agreed to play several friendlies to help accelerate United's recovery from the ravages of the Munich disaster.

**Right:** As if realizing that greater responsibility was heaped on his young shoulders after Munich, Bobby Charlton stepped up to the mark magnificently. He was United's top-scorer with 29 goals in 38 games in 1958–59; a season earlier he had been hard pressed to establish himself as a first-team regular. The pattern repeated itself at international level. Having broken into the England team in April 1958, Charlton was dropped from the World Cup squad after an indifferent performance in a 5–0 hammering by Yugoslavia just before the tournament got under way. There were concerns that for all his obvious gifts he was too much of an individualist, that his contributions were too sporadic, that he wasn't a 90-minute team player. The clamour for his recall to the international side began when England failed to win a match in Sweden, his sparkling form for United making the case unanswerable. Even Walter Winterbottom's own son took him to task over the decision to omit Charlton from the team that failed in Sweden. The 1958–59 season established Charlton as the pivotal figure in United's long road back to the top, and cemented his place in the England side, where he would remain for the next 12 years.

> **United were on the receiving end of a six-goal drubbing at the hands of Real Madrid, including two goals each from di Stefano and Puskas.**

The United squad that took the first faltering steps on the trail back to the top. Back row (l to r): Brennan, Cope, Greaves, Goodwin, Gregg, Dawson, Shiels, Foulkes, Carolan. Front row: Bradley, McGuinness, Viollet, Quixall, Charlton, Scanlon. The events in Munich meant that the precepts by which Matt Busby managed had to be put into abeyance. Meticulous planning lay at the heart of the strategy: dealing with problems before they arose and placing the emphasis on building from within. Busby once said: 'Buying players piecemeal is at best a chancy business, at worst a financial disaster. Buy them, yes. I have never had any doubts about that. But only fit them into a scheme that planning should have provided for.' The team that won back-to-back championships represented the fruits of management decisions taken years earlier. In 1953, when the reigning champions slipped to eighth in Division One,

Busby boldly pointed out to one irate board member that there was £200,000 worth of talent in the junior ranks. That talent, schooled in the United way and augmented by rare and extremely judicial purchases, had delivered two titles in majestic style. Busby knew that all sides had a limited shelf life. Five years at the top was his working estimate, though the Babes would surely have exceeded that, thanks to their early flowering. That should have afforded Busby and Jimmy Murphy the luxury of a long-term development plan for a side that would take over in the mid-sixties or thereabouts. As it was, the post-Munich period witnessed rapid internal promotions and emergency signings that were an anathema to the Busby style.

Those who contributed to the resurgent cause included left-back Joe Carolan and winger Warren Bradley. The former was yet another teenage acquisition from Dublin's Home Farm club, which had furnished

United with a number of star performers. He didn't get a first-team opportunity until after Munich, but in 1959–60 the Eire international played in 44 of the team's 45 matches. The establishment of the Brennan-Cantwell full-back partnership the following season signalled the end of his Old Trafford career and he was sold to Brighton. Amateur international winger Warren Bradley signed from Bishop Auckland just after Munich. He didn't join the professional ranks until November 1958, by which time he had turned 25. Twelve goals in 25 appearances in the second half of the 1958-59 season earned him an England call-up on 6 May 1959, when he lined up alongside Bobby Charlton against Italy at Wembley. The United pair grabbed a goal apiece in a 2–2 draw. Bradley pulled on an England shirt twice more that year but that was the extent of his international career, and by 1962 he, too, was considered surplus to requirements by Busby.

# McGuinness works his way up

Below left: Wilf McGuinness has Arsenal's outside-left Haverty jumping for safety in a league match at Highbury, 28 February 1959. McGuinness played 40 games that season, almost half the total number of appearances he made for the club. It had been United's 9–3 aggregate win over Wolves in the 1952–53 Youth Cup Final that persuaded McGuinness to join United. He took over from Duncan Edwards as captain of England Schoolboys that year, and when he saw the results United had achieved with 'lesser' players – those such as Eddie Colman, who hadn't been selected for England juniors – McGuinness was convinced Old Trafford was the place to develop his own game to its maximum potential. As a right-half he thought he wouldn't have to compete with Duncan Edwards for a place in the team, but McGuinness found himself a long-term understudy for the No. 6 shirt. There was no rancour. Like everyone else at the club, he was full of awe and respect for his clubmate. 'It wasn't like having an extra player, it was like having an extra team,' he said of the man who restricted his first-team opportunities for so long.

Below right: Fearsome forward Alex Dawson in a duel for possession during the match with the German Americans at Downing Stadium, New York, on May 15 1960. Dawson averaged more than one goal for every other league game he played throughout his four year stay at United.

Bottom: United crash out of the 1958–59 FA Cup at the first hurdle, losing 3–0 to Norwich at Carrow Road.

# Better times ahead

**Above:** The sixties side takes shape with the addition of Maurice Setters (back row, left), bought for £30,000 from West Bromwich Albion in January 1960. The first half of the 1959–60 season had exposed defensive frailties, the team having kept just one clean sheet in 26 games. Busby targeted wing-half as an issue that needed urgent attention. He had lost regular No.6 Wilf McGuinness with a broken leg, while right-half Freddie Goodwin lacked the defensive bite to go with his stylish midfield play. Finesse was not the hallmark of Setters' game, but he was a ferocious competitor. With him in the half-back line United managed six shut-outs in their last 19 fixtures that term, but Busby was just beginning. Over the next 18 months the chequebook came out again to bring Noel Cantwell, Tony Dunne and David Herd

to Old Trafford, for a modest combined total of £70,000. The new-look side didn't deliver immediately. In 1961–62 United slumped to 15th in the league, the club's worst showing since the dark days under Scott Duncan in the 1930s. But Busby had faith in the team he was building, and a run to the semi-final of the FA Cup that year gave a firm hint of better times ahead.
**Below:** Ronnie Cope and Bill Foulkes can't prevent West Ham's outside-left Malcolm Musgrove from scoring the Hammers' first goal in a League match at Upton Park, 15 April 1960. United went down 2–1. Alex Dawson was the man on target for the Reds, ending the season on a hot scoring streak of 11 goals in 10 games. With Dennis Viollet on his way to breaking United's record haul for a season, and both Charlton and Quixall also getting well into

double figures, goals weren't the problem. Indeed, United's tally of 102 in the League in 1959-60 was 19 more than the title-winners of 1955-56 bagged, and just one goal shy of the total United recorded when they retained the championship the following year. The Reds comfortably outscored the 1959-60 champions, Burnley, who found the net just 85 times. Runners-up Wolves were the only other side to notch a century that term. United's problem was at the other end. 80 goals conceded represented a worse defensive record than Luton Town, who propped up Division One that year. Busby made tightening up at the back a priority, signing Noel Cantwell from West Ham as well as Setters, though the dividend in terms of league position would not be immediate.

# Hail the arrival of The King

Matt Busby was interested in signing Denis Law when he emerged as a prodigious young talent at Huddersfield Town in the mid-1950s. Law had taken the eye playing for Huddersfield's Youth Team against United's all-conquering juniors, and Busby tabled a £10,000 offer, a huge figure for a callow 16-year-old, but it was rejected by a club that knew it had a rare talent on its books. Busby briefly doubled as Scotland manager in 1958, which afforded him his first opportunity to name Law on a team-sheet. When Huddersfield were finally willing to cash in, Law expected to become a very different Red, following Town manager Bill Shankly to Liverpool. Shanks knew that his Anfield budget wouldn't run to signing Law, an accurate assessment as the fee was a British record £55,000. Busby also held off, for different reasons. In Dennis Viollet, Albert Quixall and Bobby Charlton he had three prolific goalscorers, and it was the blue half of Manchester that secured Denis's signature. After just one full season in a struggling City side, Law joined Torino in the first transfer deal involving a British player to break the £100,000 barrier. The

Turin sojourn was also brief, unsurprisingly so. Wales and Juventus legend John Charles once said: 'Playing in Italy is just like going into one of the Services…you must tell yourself you are getting well paid and put up with the strictness and soul-destroying defensive football.' No amount of money was going to reconcile Law to a regimented lifestyle and sterile football, and he jumped at the chance to join United in the summer of 1962. His stock had risen even further, and Busby had to pay £115,000, setting another record mark, but Law had found his spiritual home. Over the next decade United fans saw the trademark raised-arm goal salute 237 times, in itself enough to make him a hero of the terraces. Add to that the swaggering exuberance, dashing verve and fiery impudence and you have the ingredients that made Law 'The King' of Old Trafford.

# Shooting star

**Below right:** Timing, technique and balance lay behind Bobby Charlton's legendary piledriver shooting. Early in his career Jimmy Murphy made him practise keeping the ball below a three-foot chalk line on a wall. This meant that if the shot was miscued slightly or struck from distance, it had every chance of flying into the top corner. Charlton scored countless goals this way, and if 'keepers managed to parry one of his rockets, the likes of Denis Law were invariably on hand to feed off the scraps. During the early sixties Charlton's expansive skills were probably appreciated more on the Continent than at home. Teams such as Barcelona and Roma – who tabled a sizeable bid – were unconditional in their admiration, while some English coaches, fellow pros and journalists criticized Charlton's tendency to drift in and out of games. He sometimes displeased his United team-mates with long raking balls that resulted in loss of possession. Murphy instilled the importance of the short game and releasing the ball early by giving him a whack on the back of his legs during training matches. Busby knew how destructive Charlton could be in the moments when he exploded into action and never showed the least inclination to sell his prize asset, while Charlton had no desire to play anywhere other than Old Trafford.

**Above right:** Dennis Viollet, Bobby Charlton and Johnny Giles launch into pre-season training as the kick-off to the 1960–61 campaign approaches. Two years on from Munich, Busby was still rebuilding. Nobby Stiles and Noel Cantwell both made their debuts that term. Stiles was a Mancunian who had signed from school, while 28-year-old Cantwell, a £29,500 buy from West Ham, already had over 250 league games under his belt. Cantwell was an inspirational leader as well as an elegant defender. The Republic of Ireland international captained United in their victory over Leicester in the 1963 FA Cup Final, and it was widely thought that he was being groomed to succeed Matt Busby. It was something of a surprise when he left Old Trafford in October 1967 to take the reins at Coventry City.

**Right inset:** Mark Pearson in action against Fulham at Craven Cottage in December 1960. Tough tackling Pearson made his first team breakthrough following the Munich tragedy.

# Bobby and Norma tie the knot

**Above right:** Club physiotherapist Ted Dalton, flanked by Wilf McGuinness and Bobby Charlton at a charity cricket match in June 1961.

**Middle right:** Bobby was a natural athlete, though he baulked when he won a place at a rugby-playing grammar school. On appeal he was allowed to transfer to Bedlington Grammar School, where the round ball game was played, and in his first year he was competing against sixth-formers.

**Below right:** Bobby is laid low with 'flu just before the FA Cup Third Round tie with Bolton, 6 January 1962. Norma Charlton's ministrations did the trick: Bobby was on the wing as usual, United running out 2–1 winners with goals from David Herd and Jimmy Nicholson. United took two other prize First Division scalps before Spurs ended their Cup run in the semi-finals, but more worrying was a league position of 15th, the club's worst showing since Busby took the managerial reins. With hindsight, some of the players felt that the tide of emotion and goodwill that had carried United in the aftermath of Munich was now exhausted. Things would get worse before they got better, for in 1962–63 United finished 19th, just three points clear of the drop zone.

**Below left:** Bobby Charlton and bride-to-be Norma Ball reading well-wishers' messages prior to their 1961 wedding, at which Maurice Setters did the best man honours. Matt Busby was a self-confessed fan of the institution of marriage, a firm believer that a stable home life was beneficial to a footballer's displays on the pitch. Affluent single men, by contrast, had a tendency for waywardness, which detracted from their performance level. His theory would be put to the test most exhaustively by George Best later in the decade.

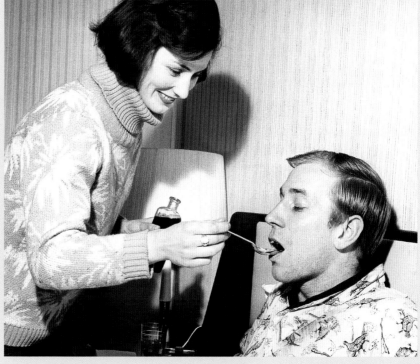

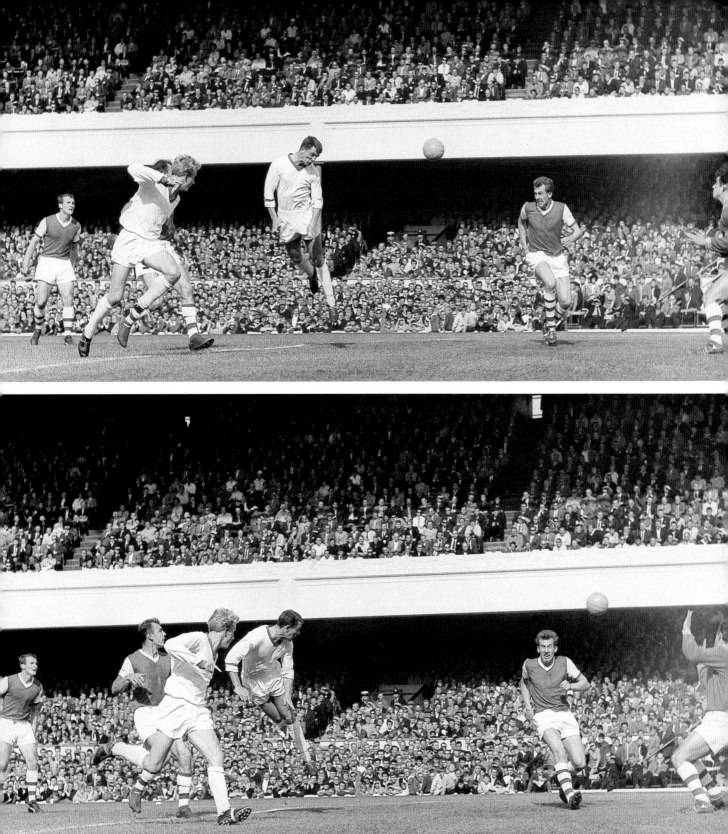

David Herd scores with a bullet header at Highbury, 25 August 1962. Herd was on target twice in a 3-1 win, the other goal coming from Phil Chisnall, a former England schoolboy international who never quite made it at United. Chisnall featured in fewer than 50 games, though he does hold a place in the record books as the last player to be involved in a direct transfer between United and Liverpool. Chisnall joined the other team in red for £25,000 in 1964. Denis Law, in his third outing in a United shirt, may not have got on the scoresheet at Highbury, but he gave a man-of-the-match performance, showing off the full array of his marvellous talents. Indeed, after netting on his debut a week earlier, Law drew a blank in the next seven games. The fans weren't worried, nor did they have need to be. By the end of the campaign the King had bagged 29 goals in 44 games.

**After scoring on his debut, Law drew a blank in the next seven games. By the end of the campaign the King had bagged 29 goals in 44 games.**

# Sadler fires United to Youth Cup victory

Below left: David Sadler behind the bar at his father's pub, the Two Brewers in Maidstone. Following the death of Sadler's mother, there was pressure on him to help out in the family concern. The pub trade held no appeal for a sports-mad youngster who was a fine cricketer as well as a target for a number of professional football clubs before he joined United.

Below right: Sixteen-year-old David Sadler and girlfriend inspect a new pair of boots for the 1962–63 season. Sadler arrived at Old Trafford that year from Isthmian League side Maidstone United, where his outstanding form had earned him a call-up to the England amateur side. He made his United debut as a 17-year-old in August 1963, though that season also saw him starring up front for the Youth Team. He hit a hat-trick in the 5–2 aggregate win over Swindon Town in the Youth Cup final, United's first victory in that competition since the Babes' five-year winning streak in the fifties. John Aston Jr and John Fitzpatrick were in that side, while George Best was drafted in at the semi-final stage, to bolster the team for a ferociously contested two-legged battle with Manchester City.

Bottom left: Jimmy Murphy felt that Dennis Viollet was never quite the same player after Munich, though he did post his best goal return two years after the crash. He broke the club record when he hit 32 goals in 36 games in 1959–60, a haul that also made him the Division One hotshot. Many were stunned when he was sold to Stoke City for £25,000 in January 1962. Still only 28, Viollet had found the net 178 times for United at a strike rate well in excess of a goal every other game. But Busby had already earmarked a younger replacement, a striker in the same quicksilver mould who would eventually overhaul Viollet's impressive tally: one Denis Law.

Bottom centre: Charlton looks at film footage of a game with Johnny Haynes.

Above right: Bobby Charlton tries his hand at goalkeeping at an England training camp. The man beaten to the ball is Sheffield Wednesday half-back Peter Swan, who lined up alongside Charlton for England on 19 consecutive occasions between 1960 and 1962. In terms of the mark they left on the game, the two men were poles apart. Charlton was the consummate sporting hero; Swan left the game in disgrace for his involvement in a match-fixing scandal in December 1962.

Bottom right: United 'Keeper Harry Gregg clears a shot over the crossbar. August 1961.

# Polished Spurs cause United to slip up

men further into the mire, but a point at Maine Road followed by a victory over Orient guaranteed the club's Division One status for another year. The manager knew he was on the right lines, for much the same team finished runners-up the following season.

**Bottom right:** Hillsborough, 31 March 1962. Spurs' Cliff Jones is on the deck as his header beats David Gaskell and Nobby Stiles in the FA Cup semi-final. United had only conceded twice in the six games it took them to reach the last four of the competition, but on the day a team in transition had to take second place to a side that showed its title-winning lustre. Spurs won the game 3-1 and went on to record the same scoreline at Wembley, with Burnley on the receiving end. Future United star John Connelly picked up a losers' medal that day. 1961-62 was the first season in which David Gaskell unseated Harry Gregg from his position as United's number one goalkeeper. As well as appearing in all the Cup games, Gaskell was between the sticks in 21 league matches, to Gregg's 13. Gaskell had waited a long time for his chance, having made his debut as a 15-year-old in the 1956 Charity Shield encounter with Manchester City. Gregg wasn't finished yet, though, and by 1964-65 Pat Dunne made it a three-way fight for the goalkeeping jersey. Gaskell played just 120 games in his 10 years at the club, the highlight of which was the 1963 FA Cup run, when he replaced Gregg for the semi-final and final.

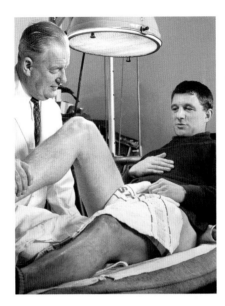

**Above right:** Maurice Setters was a player who never took a step backwards. He signed from West Bromwich Albion in January 1960 as Busby sought to plug the gaps in a leaky defence.

**Above left:** The healing hands of Ted Dalton work their magic on David Herd – this time. United's physio could do nothing to prolong Herd's Old Trafford career when the latter sustained a broken leg in 1967 playing against Leicester City, the team he scored twice against in the 1963 FA Cup Final.

**Middle right:** David Herd powers in a header to open the scoring for United in a 2-1 win over Wolves at Old Trafford, 23 April 1963. Adding two points to the total was almost as rare as hen's teeth in this dark period. The Wolves result was one of just four in the 19 League matches after the turn of the year that allowed the fans the luxury of celebrating a win. At the business end of the season Leyton Orient were adrift, with United, Manchester City and Birmingham City the other relegation contenders. Defeat at Blues put Busby's

## PART THREE

# The Belfast Boy

# Giles goes as Busby prepares to unleash Belfast wunderkind

Matt Busby allowed Johnny Giles to depart to Leeds for a bargain £37,000 in the summer of 1963, knowing that he had a fabulously gifted young Belfast boy waiting in the wings. The decision had more to do with discipline than talent, for Giles went on to enjoy an outstanding career at Elland Road. Along with Peter Beardsley, whose United career spanned half a League Cup tie in October 1982, and Frank Stapleton, who cost United a six-figure fee nine years after he was shown the door as a 16-year-old, Giles must rank among the best of 'the ones that got away' from Old Trafford. The forthright Irishman's exit followed swiftly upon his demand for an improved contract after United's Cup victory over Leicester City. Busby was somewhat parsimonious when it came to such matters, believing that pride in wearing the shirt was reward enough. It wasn't just the playing staff who found that Busby would brook no challenge to his authority. In the early days of his managerial career, Busby was publicly berated by a board member over a decision he had made. He warned his detractor never to do such a thing again,

and added 'Interference by directors' to the agenda of the next board meeting.

Below left and right: Best sports the Beatle look in 1964. The 'El Beatle' tag which catapulted him into the superstar bracket came 18 months later.

Below: 1963 The Manchester United team line-up (back row, left to right) Setters, Gaskell, Charlton, Cantwell, Foulkes, Brennan, (front row) Stiles, Law, Herd, Quixall, Crerand.

# Herd heads to United

**Above left:** In a quarter of a century as United manager, Matt Busby was hardly known for bringing players in their late 20s to the club, but he made an exception when he signed 27-year-old David Herd from Arsenal in July 1961. Busby had played alongside Herd Senior, Alex, for Manchester City in the 1930s, and father and son had set something of a record when they turned out in the same Stockport County side in the 1950–51 season. Busby's interest in the teenager dated from that time, but the Gunners stepped in then, and seven years went by before the Reds' boss got another chance to bring Herd to Old Trafford. It proved to be an inspired piece of business, for Herd continued where he left off at Highbury, hitting the net at a ratio comfortably better than a goal every other game. Indeed, 17 in 32 in his first season at the club immediately put him top of the hotshot charts, at a time when United were scarcely firing on all cylinders.

**Middle left:** David Sadler scores his first league goal for United against Everton in 1963.

**Below:** The England team gather for pre-match preparation for what will be Alf Ramsey's first match in charge as manager. John Connelly is between Jimmy Armfield on the left and Bobby Charlton. Ron Springett is far right.

**Far left:** In his debut season Denis Law fired 23 league goals, plus six in as many games during United's victorious Cup run. Despite a razor-sharp cutting edge that also included Quixall, Herd and Charlton, United flirted with the drop zone. Busby's next target was to find midfield providers who could supply the bullets for his goal aces to fire.

The Wembley disappointments of 1957 and 1958 were consigned to the history books as United revelled in the underdog's role in the 1963 FA Cup Final against Leicester City. The bitter winter created a fixture pile-up that seemed to affect United more than some other clubs, and they found themselves embroiled in a tense relegation dogfight. The Cup provided a release from the Division One grind, and as their Round Three tie against Huddersfield wasn't played until 4 March, the games came at a rate that allowed United to find some rhythm. The draw was kind. Aston Villa, Chelsea, Coventry and Southampton were next on the hit list, which meant that in reaching Wembley United had faced just one top-flight side. Leicester were a different proposition altogether, title contenders boasting the best defensive record in the division apart from champions Everton. Gordon Banks made his England debut just before the Final, but at Wembley he faced Denis Law at his imperious best (top left). He opened the scoring, and Herd grabbed a brace, with Ken Keyworth giving the Foxes small consolation ten minutes from time. The 'ragged rabble', as one newspaper dubbed the men from Manchester, were worthy winners. United had shown their quality in a six-match cup run; now they had to prove themselves in the 42-game arena. Footballers were less cosseted in 1963, though transport to Wembley was usually more luxurious than a piggyback ride. Denis Law does the donkey work for bootless Maurice Setters on Cup Final day.

**Gordon Banks made his England debut just before the Cup Final, but at Wembley he faced Denis Law at his imperious best.**

Below: The FA Cup is loaded onto a train at St. Pancras Station ready to make the journey to Manchester.

Bottom right: Matt Busby and the team make a triumphant return to Manchester with the Cup. Thousands of fans gathered outside the town hall in Albert Square to greet the players in May 1963.

Bottom left: Off the field, Tony Dunne takes a break from reading to show his black cat mascot to the cameras.

# A shift in the balance of power

Middle left: The Spurs defence is left beaten as David Herd launches himself to connect with a header at Old Trafford, 9 November 1963. Herd scored one, while Law helped himself to a hat-trick in a thumping 4-1 win. While United were rebuilding over the previous four years, Spurs hadn't finished out of the top three and had won three major cup competitions. It must have been highly satisfying to put one over on the outstanding team of the early sixties, and United repeated the trick later in the season at White Hart Lane (bottom). Busby's men finished as League runners-up, two points and two places above the Lilywhites. The balance of power was shifting. The likes of Wolves, Burnley and Leicester were fading as a Division One force, and the main threat to United would come from Bill Shankly's Liverpool side, which pipped the Reds for the championship in 1963-64, and Don Revie's Leeds, who won promotion to the top flight that season.

Above left and inset: David Herd, Billy Foulkes, Denis Law, Albert Quixall, Noel Cantwell, David Gaskell and Tony Dunne at Euston Station on 3 December 1963.

> The balance of power was shifting, and the main threat to United would come from Bill Shankly's Liverpool side and Don Revie's Leeds, who won promotion to the top flight that season.

# Best grabs headlines in sparkling debut

**Right**: 'Boy Best flashes in Red attack' ran the Manchester Evening News headline following the United–West Bromwich Albion game, 14 September 1963. It was the seventh match of the season, Ian Moir having occupied the outside-right berth for the first six. United had won four and drawn two, hardly a crisis that called for the introduction of the 17-year-old prodigy Busby had been keeping under wraps. But with Moir a fitness doubt for the West Brom game, Busby named Best as reserve. It was always his intention to play Best but he didn't want to burden the youngster with worry. He needn't have been concerned; Best gave a nerveless display in a 1–0 victory.

**Far right**: Model professional: Best's looks made him a target for fashion photographers as well as full backs. His face added to his fortune: one modelling contract with Great Universal Stores earned him a staggering £20,000.

**Below right**: Best pictured in March 1964, six months after making his debut. Busby didn't pick him again until Christmas, after United had been thumped 6–1 at Burnley. It was the reverse fixture at Old Trafford two days later, and George scored in a

sweet 5–1 victory. From that moment on he was an integral part of the first-team set-up, though he doubled up as a member of the Youth side that overcame Manchester City in the semis and Swindon in the final of the Youth Cup. It was the first time since the Babes' era that United had won the prestigious trophy; they would not do so again until Fergie's Fledglings took the honours in 1991–92.

**Below left**: George looks unconcerned as United set off for an FA Cup quarter-final replay at Sunderland. His goal at Old Trafford earned the Reds a 3–3 draw, and this game also failed to produce a winner. United took the tie 5–1 when the sides met for a third time at Huddersfield.

# Best capped after 15 games

In Best's first full season, 1964–65, he hit a respectable 14 goals in all competitions, plus numerous assists. His mesmerizing performance at Stamford Bridge on 30 September was a watershed moment, catapulting him into a different league. At the end of the game the entire crowd applauded him off the field. Both sets of players joined in, including the hapless full-back Ken Shellito, who had been run ragged for the whole 90 minutes. His rise to the top came at a dizzying pace. Before the end of his debut season he was a full international, winning his first cap in Northern Ireland's 3–2 away victory over Wales,15 April 1964. He had played just 15 League games for United.

**Above:** Pat Jennings, Laurie Brown and Denis Law pictured during a match between Tottenham Hotspur and Manchester United, October 1965.

**Below left:** Boys were smitten with George's dashing wing play; girls were smitten full stop. It wasn't long before Best had to put up with the attention of more than just enthusiastic autograph hunters.

# Pass master signs from Celtic

**Below right:** 6 February 1963. Matt Busby looks well pleased with his latest capture, Pat Crerand, a £56,000 buy from Celtic. Club secretary Les Olive and assistant manager Jimmy Murphy are also on hand to welcome to the Old Trafford fold the elegant, combative wing-half who had already been capped 11 times for Scotland. Twenty-three-year-old Crerand had been at Parkhead for six years, a fallow period in which Celtic won neither the League nor the Scottish cup. Three months after joining United he had an FA Cup winners' medal, and would add two championships and a European Cup victory to his tally before retiring in 1971. The Crerand–Stiles half-back pairing provided style and steel, the driving force behind the 1960s team and the perfect foil for the attacking artistry of Charlton, Law and Best.

**Right:** Paddy Crerand beats Fulham's Dave Metchick to the ball in a league clash at Craven Cottage early in the 1964–65 season. United lost 2–1, one of only seven defeats that term as the Reds pipped Leeds for the title. Crerand missed just three of United's 60 games that season, the heavy schedule arising from the club's run to the last four in both the FA Cup and Inter Cities Fairs Cup. Remarkably, he was nowhere near the top of the appearance chart: Foulkes, Brennan, Connelly and Tony Dunne were ever present, while Best and Charlton each missed only one game.

**Below left:** Denis Law plants a kiss on the cheek of Paddy Crerand's bride, Noreen. The couple returned to Glasgow for their wedding, which took place at the end of Crerand's first season at United. Before signing for the club he had never been to Manchester, let alone Old Trafford, and the deal was done before he had spoken a word to Matt Busby. The whole experience was something of a culture shock, and the only familiar face was that of Law, his team-mate in the Scotland team.

# Fixture pile-up takes its toll

*Right and below: panels*. Not often does a player score a hat-trick in a game and end up on the losing side, but it happened to Denis Law in the Third Round of the 1963–64 European Cup Winners' Cup. Law collected the match ball after a 4-1 win over Sporting Lisbon in the home leg, and having already put out holders Spurs, United looked a good bet to take the scalp of the Portuguese side and progress to the semis. A 5–0 reverse in Lisbon – United's worst result in European competition – meant that Busby's men were reduced to battling on just one front, for they had gone down to West Ham in the semi-final of the FA Cup on a pudding of a Hillsborough pitch four days earlier. The manager was not best pleased, though United were the victims of fixture congestion, having to play a punishing 13 games in 39 days, including three titanic FA Cup matches against Sunderland. The championship bid also fizzled out, though runners-up to Liverpool represented a huge leap forward. Law could hardly have done more: a goal a game in his 30 league outings, plus 16 more in the cups made him the club's top scorer by a distance.

*Below left*: Shortly after arriving at Old Trafford, an animated Paddy Crerand told the coaching staff of a skinny, marvellously talented boy he had watched playing for the juniors. He wasn't telling them anything they didn't already know. The sole concern was whether Best was up to the physical demands of First Division football. That was soon dispelled as Best showed he had strength and resilience to match his skill. In April 1964 he played 11 games: five first team matches, two international games and two-legged ties against both Manchester City and Swindon Town in the semi-final and final of the Youth Cup.

*Overleaf*: A Best, Law and Charlton combination in the league game with Arsenal at Highbury in 1964.

# Ground conditions

*Top* April 1965. A member of the groundstaff watches Bobby Charlton go through his paces against a backdrop of United's new North Stand, the first phase in a reconstruction process aimed at enclosing the entire stadium with a cantilever roof. The most recent development has seen the capacity rise to over 76,000, though a few more seats will have to be squeezed in to break the ground's attendance record of 76,962, set in 1939 in an FA Cup semi-final not involving United! Old Trafford may have undergone numerous facelifts since United relocated there in 1910, but even in its original guise, when three sides were open to the elements, the stadium represented a major leap forward compared with the club's first two homes. The North Road pitch in Monsall, where Newton Heath played from 1880–93, alternated between a mud bath and a concrete pad, and the players had to get changed in a public house half a mile away. The Bank Street ground in Clayton was scarcely better in terms of its playing surface, and the fans also had to contend with noxious fumes wafting from a neighbouring chemical works.

*Top above* Denis Law is surrounded by Spurs players but still comes away with the ball at White Hart Lane in 1964.

*Left middle* Nobby Stiles backs out the way while Harry Gregg punches the ball away from the Blackpool forwards in November 1965.

*Left bottom* Charlton celebrates while Fulham's Bobby Robson looks on with resignation as United score at Old Trafford in 1964.

# Record breakers

**Above:** United's stars often found themselves in opposition when they were on international duty. Here, Charlton and Law swap shirts after a hard-fought 2–2 draw between England and Scotland at Wembley on 10 April 1965. Each would end his career as his country's top marksman. By the time Charlton played his last game for England in the 1970 World Cup quarter-final defeat by West Germany, he had notched 49 goals in 106 games. The latter figure also set a new mark, Charlton breaking Billy Wright's appearance record. Since then only a handful of players have passed Charlton's mark. Law's international statistics are equally impressive. His record 30-goal haul for Scotland was subsequently equalled by Kenny Dalglish, though it took the latter 102 matches to do it; Denis got there in just 55 games.

**Above right:** 4 May 1965. Nobby Stiles gets a lift from Chelsea striker Barry Bridges during an England training session at Roehampton prior to a Wembley encounter with Hungary the following day. England won 1–0. Stiles was winning his second cap, having gained his first international outing a month earlier against Scotland, a game in which Jack Charlton also made his debut. It made the Charltons the first brothers to play for England since Nottingham Forest duo Frank and Freddie Forman in 1899. Stiles' selection had not been universally popular with football journalists but he quickly won them over by showing there was more to his game than rugged tackling. Five months before the World Cup he popped up to score the only goal of the game in what turned out to be a dress rehearsal for the final against West Germany.

**Above:** John Aston Jr attempts to fill his father's big shoes when he makes his debut against Leicester City in 1965.

# New man between the sticks

Inset below: September 1966. Alex Stepney leaves Euston for Manchester to meet his new team-mates following his £55,000 move from Chelsea, a British record fee

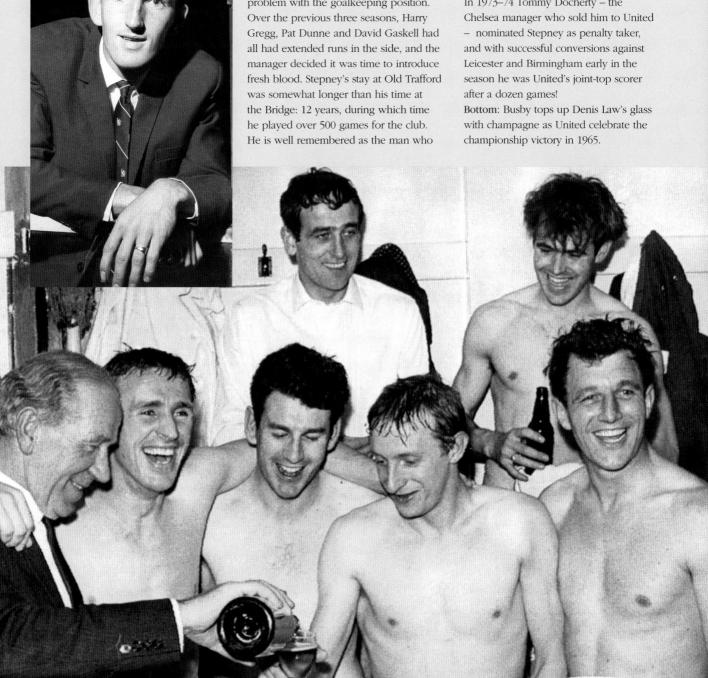

for a goalkeeper. It was something of a gamble as Stepney had built his reputation at Millwall, then a Third Division outfit. Chelsea had bought him as cover for an unsettled Peter Bonnetti, but after just four months at Stamford Bridge and a single outing, Bonnetti's problems were resolved and Stepney found himself surplus to requirements. Busby had a problem with the goalkeeping position. Over the previous three seasons, Harry Gregg, Pat Dunne and David Gaskell had all had extended runs in the side, and the manager decided it was time to introduce fresh blood. Stepney's stay at Old Trafford was somewhat longer than his time at the Bridge: 12 years, during which time he played over 500 games for the club. He is well remembered as the man who

watched a speculative punt from his Spurs counterpart Pat Jennings sail over his head in the 1967–68 Charity Shield match. He also made a costly error in the 1969–70 League Cup semi-final clash with Manchester City, spilling an indirect free kick from Francis Lee for Mike Summerbee to score the winner. But such mistakes were rare. Stepney's consistency played a crucial role in United's championship success in his first season at United, and the European Cup triumph in his second. In 1973–74 Tommy Docherty – the Chelsea manager who sold him to United – nominated Stepney as penalty taker, and with successful conversions against Leicester and Birmingham early in the season he was United's joint-top scorer after a dozen games!

**Bottom:** Busby tops up Denis Law's glass with champagne as United celebrate the championship victory in 1965.

# United champions by 0.686 of a goal

Top right: March 1965. Bill Foulkes shows off his extensive medal collection, which he hoped to add to as United were battling on three fronts at the end of the 1964-5 season. The Reds won through to their fourth successive FA Cup semi-final but went down to Leeds after two titanic battles. They fell at the same hurdle in the Fairs Cup, to Hungarian side Ferencvaros. United had banged in 25 goals in reaching the last four, including a 10-goal avalanche against a Borussia Dortmund side that had been European Cup semi-finalists the year before. The Ferencvaros tie was all square after two matches, and in the days before away goals counted, the flip of a coin decided the venue for a third game. The Hungarian side won the toss and the game, which was played on 16 June. After 60 games and 10 long months, United's champagne season finally lost its fizz, though the championship trophy was back in the Old Trafford trophy room after an eight-year absence.

Middle right: Bobby Charlton lived and breathed football, so his choice of reading material to share with daughter Suzanne was hardly surprising. Note the non-PC title, a reflection of the prevailing attitude of the time. Suzanne would become a media celebrity in her own right as a TV weather presenter.

Below right: City rivalry is briefly put aside as Matt Busby attends a civic reception marking Manchester City's return to the top flight after winning the Second Division championship in 1965–66. Derby matches were back on the agenda for the first time since

1962–63, when City lost a relegation dogfight that included United. Busby is pictured chatting to City skipper Johnny Crossan, his wife Barbara and Maine Road boss Joe Mercer.

Below middle: Denis Law and Tony Dunne practise their goal celebration.

Below left: John Connelly spent just two years at Old Trafford but made a vital contribution to the mid-sixties side. An international-class winger who featured in two World Cup campaigns, Connelly had won League and FA Cup winners' medals with Burnley before arriving at Old Trafford in a £60,000 deal in April 1964. He scored one of the most crucial goals in the club's history, at Elland Road in the title run-in to the 1964–65 season. United had already faced Leeds three times – at Old Trafford in the League and in an FA Cup tie that went to a replay – without registering a goal. Connelly's winner at Leeds proved crucial as United edged Don Revie's outfit for the championship on goal average, albeit a wafer-thin margin of 0.686. Connelly and Best helped themselves to 25 league goals between them, as well as helping supply 58 for Law, Charlton and Herd. Charlton was now parading his skills in a deep-lying central role, a positional move replicated in the national side. Connelly was one of the casualties when the England boss introduced his 'wingless wonders' policy in 1966, though he did play in the drawn opening group match against Uruguay. There was some surprise when United sold him to Division Two side Blackburn Rovers two months after the World Cup triumph.

George Best in action against Wolves in a fifth round FA Cup tie at Molineux, 5 March 1966. Best scored the pick of the goals in a 4–2 victory for the Reds, but it was his performance against Benfica at the Stadium of Light four days later that established him as one of Europe's top players. United went into their European Cup tie in Lisbon holding a narrow 3–2 advantage and Matt Busby told his men to keep things tight for the first 20 minutes. George had other ideas, for by then United were 3–0 up. He scored twice in a stunning 5–1 victory which sent shockwaves throughout the Continent. To put the result in perspective, Benfica had enjoyed a run of 18 consecutive home wins in European competition, scoring 78 goals and conceding just 14. No visiting team had scored more than twice in fortress Lisbon.

11 April 1966. With a European Cup semi-final against Partizan Belgrade just 48 hours away, United physio Ted Dalton's healing hands are working overtime on George Best. He was carrying a cartilage injury from a nasty tackle in an FA Cup quarter-final tie against Preston a fortnight before, but Busby could ill afford to let him have the operation he needed. A top three place in the league to guarantee entry into the Fairs Cup was vital, though, naturally, Busby hoped to be in the European Cup as holders. Best was given a run-out in a league match against Leicester, which United lost, and Busby decided to gamble. George was strapped up and sent out onto the pitch, but broke down during the game and became a passenger. United lost the match 2–0. Even without Best – whose season was over – United were confident of turning the tie around at Old Trafford, but Partizan mounted a sturdy rearguard. Stiles pulled one back, but United must have known it wasn't to be their night when Nobby threw a punch at an opponent, only for a confused referee to give Crerand his marching orders. After beating star-studded Benfica, United had gone out to a workmanlike East European side. And to make matters worse, United finished fourth in the league, so it would be at least two years before they could try once again to conquer the European summit.

# 'El Beatle' bid for pop stardom stymied

Right: Best gets the maternal treatment from landlady Mary Fullaway, at whose Chorlton-cum-Hardy house he lodged, intermittently, for 10 years. David Sadler arrived as a house guest at around the same time, and the two became firm friends, but the experiences of the two men who shot to fame as 17-year-olds just as the sixties started to swing could hardly have been more different. Best was the cavalier with the dashing good looks, always in the spotlight. The temptation to burn the candle at both ends was irresistible, and in the early stages of his career the carousing had no detrimental effect on his performances on the pitch.

Below: In 1966 talks reached an advanced stage for George Best to cut a record before Matt Busby stepped in and vetoed the deal. Busby felt that the two careers wouldn't mix and Best's football would suffer. The manager won that battle, though he couldn't prevent Best living the pop star lifestyle to the full.

Best remained a shy Belfast boy at heart, and alcohol no doubt helped him deal with the attention he received on the social circuit. He never developed a taste for beer. Vodka and lemonade – sweet-tasting but nonetheless potent – became a favourite tipple. Busby dispensed the first of many slaps on the wrist early in the

> The temptation to burn the candle at both ends was irresistible, and in the early stages of his career the carousing had no detrimental effect on Best's performances on the pitch.

1965–66 season, dropping Best after a poor start to the campaign. It didn't last long. He was an indulgent patriarch, ever willing to forgive his superstar's transgressions. He was also a shrewd manager who wanted his match-winner terrorizing defenders out on the pitch.

# The best way to defend against George: play on the opposite flank

Perfect balance and control were among the hallmarks of George Best's game, demonstrated admirably here in a 3–1 win at Chelsea, 5 November 1966. Scotland international Eddie McCreadie is the defender on the receiving end on this occasion. McCreadie was a stalwart in Chelsea's attractive sixties side, but soon learned that facing Best was an unrewarding, if not humiliating, experience. A year later, he lined up for Scotland against Northern Ireland at Windsor Park and found, no doubt much to his relief, that Best was on the opposite flank. In what was, by common consent, the greatest performance of his 37-match international career, Best took on the entire Scotland team virtually single-handed, and created the chance from which David Clements scored the game's only goal. At right-back that day was Celtic's Tommy Gemmell. He was soon to be immortalized as one of the Lisbon Lions, but that day he cut a tormented and bemused figure. At half-time Gemmell invited McCreadie to swap sides with him. The Chelsea defender declined the offer.

# Three-pronged attack tests Busby stars

Far right: The ever consistent, ever reliable Tony Dunne clocked up over 500 games for United. He and Shay Brennan – his full-back partner through much of the golden sixties period – were speedy and skilful defenders in the Roger Byrne mould.

Right: 12 March 1966. Three days after the memorable 5–1 away victory over Benfica in the quarter-final of the European Cup, the same United side found itself 2–0 down inside five minutes against Chelsea at Stamford Bridge. Here, John Hollins foils David Herd's attempt to get United back into the match. There was no further scoring in the game, one of only nine in the team's 57-match season in which the potent forward line failed to find the net. As had happened in 1963–64, United battled hard on three fronts only to end the season empty-handed. The club began the season with 14 internationals on its books, plus David Sadler, an England amateur cap, but Busby's reserves were tested to the limit and came up fractionally short in the three competitions.

Middle: Bobby Charlton sells Blackpool 'keeper Tony Waiters a delightful dummy before scoring in a 2–1 league victory at Old Trafford, 27 April 1966. He made United's other goal, Law heading home from his pinpoint driven cross. Charlton's virtuosity raised the spirits of a jaded-looking side that had lost two semi-finals in the previous week. Following the shock 2–1 aggregate defeat to Partizan Belgrade in the European Cup, United went down 1–0 to Everton in the FA

Cup. Colin Harvey's goal completed an agonizing hat-trick for United, who had lost three semi-finals in a row since lifting the trophy in 1963.

Below: The United goalkeeper, Alex Stepney saves a shot during training. He was the subject of two transfer deals within four months. After

Chelsea had bought him from Millwall for £50,000, United bought him from Chelsea for £55,000.

# Charlton tops European poll

Middle left: Bobby Charlton and family pictured in 1966, when Charlton picked up the European Footballer of the Year award. He also picked up the domestic award, given by the Football Writers, beating George Cohen and George Best by some margin. Denis Law had been named European Footballer of the Year two years earlier, while George Best would win the award in 1968. Only twice since has a player with an English club won the award – Michael Owen in 2001 and Ronaldo in 2008 – though Kevin Keegan did take Europe's top individual honour twice in the late 1970s while playing for SV Hamburg.

Middle right: Nobby Stiles racks up yet another fine from the FA Disciplinary Committee, this time for a sending off in a pre-season friendly prior to the 1966–67 campaign. A show of 'ungentlemanly conduct' towards the referee who gave him his marching orders cost Stiles £50. The combative midfielder was a vital cog in the great 1960s side, a terrier-like man-marker who provided excellent defensive cover. His uncompromising style led to calls for him to be dropped from the England side in the early stages of the 1966 World Cup campaign. Alf Ramsey wisely ignored them. Stiles, Best and Law felt the sharp end of many a referee's tongue, but they were angelic compared to Frank Barson, a United stalwart of the 1920s. A former blacksmith, Barson was as hard as an anvil and a fearsome competitor. He was sent off 12 times and is said to have served more suspensions than any player in the game's history. He once served a two-month ban for rendering a Manchester City player unconscious, and spent over six months on the sidelines in a single season for on-field misdemeanours during a spell at Watford. Barson was a highly effective central defender, though, a member of England's one-cap wonder brigade. Barson joined United after the club had been relegated in 1921–22, and was promised a public house if he could help get the team back in the top flight within three years. Promotion came in the third season and Barson duly got his pub. But this bluff Yorkshireman decided within an hour that the attention of back-slapping well-wishers wasn't for him and handed the keys to his head barman.

Top right: Nobby Stiles wields the willow in the glorious summer of 1966, when he added a World Cup winners' medal to his collection. Note the glasses for improved hand-eye co-ordination. Stiles' eyesight was extremely poor, and until he took to wearing contact lenses, it was often said he didn't so much tackle opponents as collide with them.

Bottom: November 1966. Bobby Charlton and Nobby Stiles at the launch of Jack Charlton's new business venture, a men's outfitter's in Garforth, near Leeds. Linking the two United stars is Jack's wife, Pat. The traditional United – Leeds rivalry dates from this era, the teams locking horns in numerous attritional battles. With the likes of Bobby Collins, Billy Bremner, Norman Hunter and Big Jack himself coming up against United's pugnacious contingent, the games were invariably punctuated with flare-ups.

# Herd instinct

Above right: David Herd, Bobby Charlton, Shay Brennan and Nobby Stiles relaxing in the capital prior to the league clash with West Ham at Upton Park on 30 April 1966. Noel Cantwell and John Aston scored but United went down 3–2 to a team that was about to boast three World Cup winners. United took six points from their last four games but had to cede the league crown to Liverpool. For David Herd, the man with a rocket shot timed at 72 mph, this would be the last full campaign. After plundering 32 goals in all competitions this term, Herd sustained a broken leg during the run-in the following year, an injury which effectively curtailed his Old Trafford career. He played just six League matches in 1967–68, and featured in only one of the nine games that culminated in the glorious Wembley triumph over Benfica, but he rightfully received a European Cup winners' medal to add to the FA Cup and two championship winners' medals he picked up during his seven years at the club. Herd had to live in the shadow of the great triumvirate of the day, and his enormous contribution to the success United enjoyed in the sixties rarely gets the plaudits it deserves. He joined Stoke City in July 1968, and had a brief spell in management with Lincoln City before quitting the game in the early seventies.
Above left: George's flair extended beyond the football pitch. He started designing clothes in the mid-sixties, which provided even more opportunities for liaisons with leggy blonde models.
Right: Denis Law playing for Scotland in 1967 as they beat England for the first time since the old enemy had won the World Cup less than one year earlier.

Above left: Like George Best, Mike Summerbee was a formidable competitor, possibly the only player in the history of the game to be sent off in a testimonial. He, too, was an entertainer on the pitch and a party animal off it, and the two became firm friends following Summerbee's arrival at Maine Road from Swindon. George was best man at Summerbee's wedding, and the two became business partners, opening a boutique. In the pressure-cooker derbies the pair often staged a joke set piece early in the game, then spent the rest of the 90 minutes terrorizing the full-backs they were up against. Summerbee was placed in an awkward position when Best was involved in the leg-breaking tackle which effectively ended City star Glyn Pardoe's career in December 1970, for the rest of the Blues were incensed at what they regarded as a reckless challenge.

Above right: Bill Foulkes finds out what the papers have to say about United's chances in the game at Stamford Bridge, 12 March 1966. Chelsea won 2–0, denting United's hopes of retaining the championship. It was one of only nine defeats that term – only Liverpool bettered that – but United drew 15 matches, more than any other team in the division that season. Eight of those came at Old Trafford, dropped points which proved costly as champions Liverpool finished 10 points ahead of the Reds.

Below: A disconsolate Nobby Stiles as United lose the 1966 FA Cup semi final to Everton.

# Top honours for United men

Top: August 1967. United players toast Matt Busby as he is made a Freeman of the City of Manchester. He was awarded a CBE in 1958, and a knighthood following United's European Cup triumph a decade later. In 2002 he was posthumously inducted into English football's Hall of Fame in its inaugural year. Of the original 29-strong list, eight had a United connection. Six were players – Best, Cantona, Charlton, Edwards, Law and Robson – while Busby and Ferguson were among only six managers named.

Right and above inset: Stiles, Charlton and Best celebrating at an awards dinner.

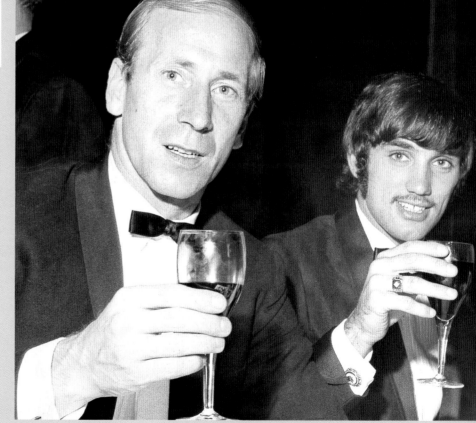

# Busby masterminds fifth championship success

Above: Applause all round as United lift the 1966–67 league title, the seventh championship in the club's history and fifth in the Busby era. United held off the challenge of surprise contenders Nottingham Forest – managed by Old Trafford legend Johnny Carey – Spurs and Leeds. The championship was clinched in style, with a 6–1 win at Upton Park in the penultimate fixture of the campaign. This success put United level with Arsenal and Liverpool in the record books, though both of those clubs, and Everton, would forge ahead over the next 25 years. However, thirteen championship titles since the inception of the Premier League has redressed that situation.

Right: David Sadler gave assured and consistent performances in the centre of United's defence for a decade, though one of the highlights of his career came in the semi-final of the 1967–68 European Cup, when he reverted to the role of striker. United were trailing Real Madrid 3–1 at the Bernabeu Stadium – 3–2 on aggregate – when Sadler headed in a Crerand free kick to level the score. Sadler had scored plenty of goals in the early part of his career, and knew where the goal was. The winner came from a much more unlikely source, Bill Foulkes, who scored just nine times in his 18 years at Old Trafford.

# Legends at loggerheads

Right: There was a natural affinity between Law and Best, who shared a streak of devilment as well as great footballing gifts. Law may have been The King, but he humbly deferred to Best's talents. 'From 1964 to 1969 he was the best in the country.'

Below: Best shields the ball as another crunching tackle comes in from behind. A facet of his game sometimes overlooked is the fearlessness and resilience with which he faced scything challenges from defenders who were granted much more licence to make their mark than their present-day counterparts.

Law may have been The King, but he humbly deferred to Best's talents. 'From 1964 to 1969 he was the best in the country.'

Right: Bobby Charlton was the consummate professional, a footballer of exemplary conduct both on the field and off, someone who never cut corners in training or did anything that might compromise the success of the team. He was never particularly close to George Best, and their relationship worsened when the latter started to go off the rails. For his part, Best felt that Charlton was too fond of showboating with long raking passes which too often went astray. It reached a point when the two were barely on speaking terms, one of many divisions that afflicted United in the years following the European Cup success.

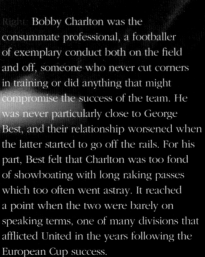

# And he was good in the air, too…

Above: There was no relief for defenders if United took the aerial route to pick out George Best, for his terrific spring made him as much a danger in the air as on the deck. His temperament may have made him a liability at times, but Best ticked every box in the skills department. David Sadler – who was himself one of the most sought-after youngsters in the land and one of a host of full internationals on United's books – once remarked that at the height of his powers George could have turned out in any position on the field and outperformed the usual incumbent.

At the age of 20 Best had the world at his feet. At 22 he won both the domestic and European Footballer of the Year awards, the then youngest player to be honoured by either of those bodies. He had much left to offer, but by common consensus the side peaked in 1966, although it won the League title and European crown in the following two seasons. Best's struggle to come to terms with the decline was a significant factor in his aberrant behaviour during the five-year period following the Wembley victory over Benfica.

Left: Nobby Stiles and Jimmy Greaves in 1966.

# United lose out in title showdown

Right: Bobby Charlton training with England in 1967.

Far right: Bill Foulkes and David Sadler swap ideas over the tactics board as they prepare to face the twin threat of Southampton's Ron Davies and Martin Chivers at Old Trafford, 17 November 1967. The United defence was breached twice, but goals from Charlton, Kidd and Aston kept the team on track to retain the championship. Sadler was seen as the man who would eventually step into Foulkes' boots at centre-half, though the 21-year-old said he was still the apprentice, Foulkes the master. The widespread view was that Sadler would enjoy a longer international career than the unlucky Foulkes, but with Brian Labone, Jack Charlton or Roy McFarland partnering Bobby Moore, opportunities at the heart of the England defence were restricted. Sadler won four caps, just three more than his United team-mate.

Middle left: David Sadler pictured in November 1967.

Middle right: Bill Foulkes called it a day at the end of the 1969–70 season, by which time he had turned 38. The man bought to replace him, Arsenal's Ian Ure, was a pale imitation of the legendary Foulkes, a player who failed to win over the fans in his brief spell at Old Trafford.

Bottom: August 1967. Matt Busby watches the squad go through their paces as United gear up to defend their league crown.

It began with an opening-day defeat at Goodison Park, but the team lost just twice more before the turn of the year and headed the table. By Easter United were vying with regular contenders Leeds and Liverpool along with Manchester City, who had finished 15th the previous season. At the shake-up it was a straight fight between the two Manchester clubs, and City had it in their own hands. No doubt with half an eye on the European Cup, United went down at home to Sunderland – one of seven defeats in the last three months of the season – though it made no difference as City won their final game and clinched the title.

The Manchester Evening News had two alternative headlines ready to roll off the presses, and it is said that right up to the last minute the editor – a die-hard Reds fan – refused to ditch the 'United Champions' version, hoping for a late miracle.

# Astute wing-half

Right: Matt Busby had an understanding with Celtic that United should be offered first refusal on Pat Crerand if the midfielder became available. Busby was also interested in Rangers' Jim Baxter at the time, but Denis Law (middle right), who knew both players well from international duty, advised that Crerand's astute wing-half play would serve the team better than Baxter's extravagant individual skills.

Far right: Harry Gregg between the sticks against Wolves at Molineux.

Below right: 18 year-old Brian Kidd heads wide of the net as Spurs goalkeeper Pat Jennings and central defender Mike England watch helplessly as the ball sails over the bar.

Below left: Shay Brennan in May 1968.

Bottom: A collision of one of his players with George Best causes concern to Bobby Moore in the game between United and West Ham in 1967.

# Best steps up to the goalscoring plate

Top right: February 1968. George shows off his latest girlfriend. On the field this was to be the zenith of Best's career. He hit 28 goals from 41 League outings; Charlton and Kidd were next in United's goalscoring order of merit, on 15 apiece. Best's tally put him level with Southampton and Wales striker Ron Davies, the two men sharing the Golden Boot award for the top flight's ace marksman. Best also scored three times in the European Cup, and was on target in the Third Round FA Cup clash against Spurs, which United lost in a replay. Injuries to David Herd and Denis Law – who had been veritable goal machines for the past five years – prompted Busby to enquire about the availability of World Cup hero Geoff Hurst and Celtic wing magician

Jimmy Johnstone. Those came to nothing, and in the event the manager's concerns about the lack of firepower were answered emphatically from within.

Below: Best's iconic status at United stretched far beyond the terraces and the attention of autograph-hunting fans. Successive generations of players, including Sammy McIlroy, Ryan Giggs and Cristiano Ronaldo, have had to contend with 'the new George Best' tag.

Right middle: The most famous locks in football get the personal touch at the Chorlton-cum-Hardy digs, with David Sadler looking on. For extra-curricular activities beyond the watchful eye of landlady Mary Fullaway, George rented a pied-a-terre with fellow roisterer Mike Summerbee.

Successive generations of players, including Sammy McIlroy, Ryan Giggs and Cristiano Ronaldo, have had to contend with 'the new George Best' tag.

# Third United player scoops Writers' poll

Bottom: 16 May 1968. George Best follows in the footsteps of Johnny Carey and Bobby Charlton as he is named Football Writers' Footballer of the Year. Everton's Brian Labone and Leeds' Billy Bremner were in contention for the award, but Best's scintillating season for club and country made it a one-horse race. It would be another 28 years before another United player picked up that honour, King Eric scooping the poll in 1996. Roy Keane (2000), Teddy Sheringham (2001), Cristiano Ronaldo (2007 and 2008) and Wayne Rooney (2010) have since swelled the ranks of United winners of the award to eight.

Above right: Willie Morgan hitches a ride on George Best's back, a fitting image as the latter increasingly felt he was carrying the team. The Burnley and Scotland winger, bought for £100,000 in the summer of 1968,

might have had the Best look, but George was unimpressed with the efforts made to improve the team after the European Cup success. Morgan, who was Sir Matt's sole purchase during that close season, was popular on the terraces, however; a raiding winger who saw United through the dark days of relegation and the triumphant return to the First Division in 1975. Tommy Docherty conferred the captaincy on him, which must have irked Best still further at a time when he felt the side should have been rebuilt around him.

Below right: A fondness for alcohol and fast cars was a dangerous mix that inevitably threatened to land Best in hot water. Hours before United took on City in a crucial League match at Old Trafford on 27 March 1968, George was in court on a careless driving charge. He had written off his Jaguar in a crash the previous December – and immediately replaced it with a new S-type. United lost the derby 3–1, a result which turned the title race in favour of the Blue half of the city.

Below inset: When all was going well on the pitch, Best's glamour-boy pursuits, including lucrative modelling assignments, presented no problem. But when the team began to struggle and George began to go awol, it had a damaging effect on morale.

# The Cup that didn't overflow with kindness

Bottom left: Two-year-old Lorraine Crerand watches as her dad is patched up by United physio Ted Dalton, with trainer and former 'keeper Jack Crompton looking on. The repair work was necessitated by the bruising encounter with Estudiantes in the World Club Cup. Both matches were incendiary affairs, and predictably so. The dirty tricks were in evidence even before the kick-off in Buenos Aires, as the lifts to United's 16th floor hotel accommodation were mysteriously out of commission for the duration of United's stay. On the pitch Busby's men showed commendable restraint in the 1–0 defeat, though Stiles was

given his marching orders for questioning a linesman's decision. At Old Trafford the South Americans doubled their lead with a goal from Ramon Veron, father of Juan Sebastian. Willie Morgan pulled one back, by which time it was 10 v 10, Best and Medina having been sent off for fighting. Brian Kidd thought he'd tied the scores on the stroke of full-time, only for the referee to claim he'd blown before the ball crossed the line. United had lost but it was hardly a major blow, for the prospect of a third bloodbath against a side that flouted the spirit of the game was distinctly unappealing.

Left: Matt Busby may have played for two of United's greatest rivals, Manchester City and Liverpool, but from 1945 until his death in 1994, he was a Red through and through. Indeed, Busby coined the name 'Red Devils' in the early 1960s, appropriating it from Salford Rugby League Club.

Above right: March 1968. Nobby takes advantage of a mid-season break to practise his swing.

Middle right: A new addition to the Stiles' household, named Robert Francis, after Messrs Charlton and Burns.

Bottom right: A star-struck Red claims a prize 'royal' signature midway through the 1967–68 season. Ten years on from Munich, this European Cup-winning campaign would represent the pinnacle of the Busby era, but for the King it was a frustrating campaign. A knee injury restricted him to a handful of league appearances, and he was forced to watch the Wembley showdown with Benfica from a hospital bed.

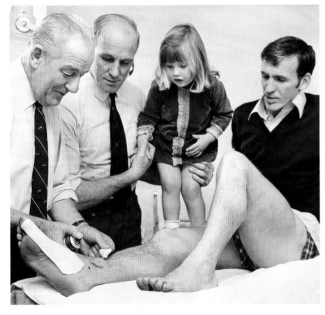

# Cup defeat a blessing

Top right: Brian Kidd was a product of St Patrick's School, Collyhurst, the seat of learning that had also produced Wilf McGuinness and Nobby Stiles. All strikers need the ability to time their runs, and Kidd did so perfectly as he was promoted to the first team at the beginning of the 1967–68 season to fill the gap vacated by the injured David Herd. Eighteen-year-old Kidd scored 15 League goals in 38 games, and notched two more in the European Cup run, the second of which came in the Wembley final. Scoring in European football's glamour showpiece on the stroke of turning 19 was always going to be a hard act to follow, and although Kidd gave superb service to United for another six years, and enjoyed successful spells at Arsenal, Everton and Bolton, his debut season at Old Trafford produced his finest hour.

Middle right: 3 February 1968. Brian Kidd in action at White Hart Lane in a league match which United won 2–1. It was the third time in eight days the teams had met, Spurs coming out on top in an FA Cup tie that went to a replay. Over 177,000 watched the three games involving two of the most attractive sides in the country. With hindsight, some of the players thought the early Cup exit the previous year had been a blessing in disguise, allowing United to target their efforts on winning the championship. Defeat by Spurs at the first hurdle this time round enabled the team to focus on two fronts: retaining the title and lifting the European Cup. They came agonizingly close to completing that double.

Below right: Five years before his famous double save against Leeds in the FA Cup final, Sunderland's Jim Montgomery gathers safely at the feet of Brian Kidd. United went into this match – the last league game of the 1967–68 season – level on points with Manchester City but with an inferior goal average.  They needed at least a point to have any chance of retaining the championship, but lowly Sunderland left Old Trafford with the spoils and United fans had no need to check to see how their city rivals had fared at Newcastle. Perhaps United took their eye off the ball, for they were due to face Real Madrid at the Bernabeu Stadium in a European Cup semi-final four days later. As it was, City won at St James's Park, making the Sunderland result academic.

Bottom: Bobby Charlton and Paddy Crerand each played in 52 of the United's 53 League and Cup matches in 1967–68, as did Alex Stepney and George Best. Three other players, Tony Dunne, Brian Kidd and David Sadler, were ever present on the European Cup trail, giving the side a settled spine. Perhaps the unluckiest man was Francis Burns, who had been Dunne's full-back partner for most of the season, only to lose out to Shay Brennan in the selection shake-up for Wembley. For Brennan the wheel of fortune had come full circle, for he had lost out to Dunne and Cantwell in the 1963 FA Cup Final, having partnered one or other of them for much of that campaign.

Middle left: A despondent Bill Foulkes leaves the training pitch after losing his race to be fit for the FA Cup replay against Spurs. David Sadler proved to be an able deputy that night and for the majority of the remaining games of the season. Both men were fit for the European Cup Final, giving Busby a potential selection quandary, but an injury to Denis Law allowed him to deploy Sadler up front.

# Booking confirmed – 32 years after match!

**Right and below left:** Two of the most gifted footballers the game has produced, George Best (right) and Bobby Charlton (below left). They handled fame and the trappings of success very differently. The words 'Bobby Charlton' were synonymous with English football and uttered by soccer fans in far-flung locations who couldn't speak another word of the language. Even at the height of his playing days, Charlton comported himself with total dignity, the game's finest ambassador long before that role was bestowed upon him. Bobby would have subscribed to the view held by his manager: 'Winning isn't the test of real achievement. There should be no conceit in victory and no despair in defeat.' Consider the evidence of his disciplinary record: 754 appearances for United and 106 for his country, with just two minor blips on the charge sheet. One of those came in the 1967 Charity Shield encounter with Spurs, Charlton booked for time-wasting when United were 3–2 down! Common sense prevailed and it was later expunged from the record books. A second caution didn't come to light until 1998, more than 20 years after Bobby had hung up his boots. It was awarded during one of the many scuffles during the infamous England-Argentina clash at the 1966 World Cup. Charlton intervened as peacemaker but had his name taken without realizing it, a regular occurrence before colour-coded cards were introduced. Indeed, the opacity of that incident led English official Ken Aston to devise the traffic-light system, introduced at the Mexico tournament four years later.

**Below right:** George Best and Jimmy Ryan have a satisfied air following a tricky but ultimately victorious away trip to Gornik Zabrze in the 1967–68 European Cup quarter-final. The Polish champions had beaten Dynamo Kiev, who in turn had knocked out holders Celtic, and were tipped by some as an outside bet to go all the way in the competition. United took a 2–0 lead to Poland, and needed that cushion as they went down to a goal from star striker Lubanski. In freezing conditions Busby had opted for a cautious approach, drafting in John Fitzpatrick for Ryan, a tactic which paid off handsomely. United had lost the match but were through to a fourth European Cup semi-final.

# Best on target against Real Madrid

Right and bottom: Old Trafford, 24 April 1968. Embraces all round after George Best lashes in John Aston's pass half-an-hour into the European Cup semi-final clash with Real Madrid. United couldn't breach the Spanish giants' defence again and the visitors were more than satisfied to take a 1–0 deficit back to the Bernabeu Stadium. Foulkes for the injured Law was the only personnel change for the return, and it was the veteran defender's goal that settled the tie.

**Middle right:** Bobby Charlton became England's all-time leading scorer when he netted in a 3–1 win over Sweden at Wembley, 22 May 1968, a week before United faced Benfica in the European Cup final. That strike, in his 85th game, put Charlton on 45, one clear of Jimmy Greaves. He would add four more to his tally before his international career ended, his last coming against Colombia in a World Cup 1970 warm-up match. Gary Lineker's 48-goal haul is the closest anyone has come to reaching Charlton's mark.

**Middle left:** George Best in action during the 1968–69 season, when he once again topped the scoring chart for United. His 19 League goals represented exactly one-third of United's total, the club's poorest attacking display since the 1930s.

# Best falls foul of the law

**Above left:** George Best was always newsworthy, a prime target for the snap-happy press corps and as likely to be found on the front page as the sports section. A six-month driving ban imposed in 1968 provided an ideal photo-opportunity for George to show off his alternative means of transport. Pop-star celebrity and a large disposable income has caused problems for a number of players over the years, even though the phenomenon is now well understood and advisers are on hand. Best blazed the trail single-handedly, and it was hardly surprising that the pressures took their toll.

**Middle left:** The birthday boy got the present he could scarcely have wished for five years after signing schoolboy forms at the age of 14. Scoring for United in a Wembley final was a dream for the young Brian Kidd, who, like so many before and since, was an avid supporter before becoming a player.

**Above right:** Like David Herd, the man he replaced in the United side, Brian Kidd was a powerful centre-forward who could deliver a stinging shot. His conversion rate during his time at Old Trafford wasn't quite in Herd's class – a little better than a goal every four games – but he made a valuable contribution at a time when United were on a downward curve. His international stats were better: one goal in two, though he did get just two outings in the Ramsey era, both in the run-up to the 1970 World Cup.

**Below left and right:** George clocks up a different kind of hat-trick while holidaying in Majorca in the summer of 1968. It was back to Manchester with a bump shortly afterwards as much the same side that had won the European Cup made a patchy start to the 1968–69 season. The team that had swept to the title in 1966–67 lost just six games; two years on United clocked up as many defeats before October was out. Sir Matt knew that changes would have to be made, and, as he was approaching his 60th birthday, perhaps felt that the emotional as well as practical upheaval of dismantling his third great side was best left to someone else. Best should have been the cornerstone of any redevelopment plans, but he and his manager found themselves in a chicken-and-egg situation when the rot set in. George insisted he would settle down if he were given the captaincy and the team was rebuilt around him. Busby demanded that he show a more responsible attitude first, an uneasy stand-off that persisted with Busby's successors.

## PART FOUR

# Champions of Europe

# United edge a step nearer Holy Grail

**Above**: Matt Busby tells his players exactly what he wants of them when they take the field against Benfica. He had to lift the team after the disappointment of ceding the league crown to their City neighbours. United had had a five-point cushion at one stage, but seven defeats in the last 15 games allowed Manchester City to pip them for the title by two points. When the clubs contested their 100th league derby in March 1980 – a game decided by a Mickey Thomas goal – the record books showed a fairly even division of the spoils: 37 wins for United, 30 for City, with 33 draws. Remarkably, they had scored 140 goals each. Since then, United have pulled away, not just in terms of head-to-head meetings but in the small matter of silverware. The Reds have added 24 domestic and three European trophies to the cabinet, plus assorted successes in the European Super Cup and Charity Shield. City's cupboard remained bare for 35 years following their League Cup victory of 1976, but Abu Dhabi funding and a "Galactico" recruitment drive delivered the FA Cup and league title in quick succession. Sir Alex responded by signing Robin van Persie as he set about silencing the "noisy neighbours" in 2012-13, putting United back on top of the pile in what would be his last campaign.

**Opposite top**: Even at 59 Matt Busby shows a sprightly turn of foot as he referees a practice match during the team's preparations for the European Cup Final. Busby had been an average inside-forward who struggled to make an impact at Manchester City in the early 1930s. After converting to wing-half, Busby became one of the great players of the prewar era. He appeared in consecutive Cup Finals, picking up a winners' medal in 1934, the year he won his only cap for Scotland. Joe Mercer, who locked horns with Busby both as a player and as manager of City in the 1960s, described him as 'a player's player who influenced everything around him'.

**Below**: Matt Busby has barely set foot off the plane before a congratulatory hand is proffered. Felicitations were certainly in order, as United had just fought out a 3–3 draw in the cauldron of the Bernabeu Stadium, a result which gave United a 4–3 aggregate victory over Real Madrid and passage through to the European Cup Final.

# Fulfilment of a dream

Above and right: Besuited and sporting sunglasses, Matt Busby exudes a sense of calm as he prepares the team to face Benfica at Wembley on 29 May. The task was formidable, for the Portuguese giants were appearing in their fifth final in eight years, and in Eusebio boasted Europe's current Golden Boot winner. But Busby knew his team – the third great championship-winning side he had built – had the wherewithal to replicate the famous victory recorded in Lisbon two years before. Seven of that side featured in the 1968 showpiece. Gregg, Herd and Connelly had gone, while Law was injured. Stepney, Sadler, Aston and Kidd – celebrating his 19th birthday – were the players not involved in the quarter-final clash two years earlier. Busby scented victory for a different reason. 'Their heart is right, and that is the important thing,' said the manager during final preparations for the big game.

# Fulfilment of a dream

Opposite above: Disappointed supporters, unable to buy tickets for the Final, sit outside Wembley Stadium (inset) while those inside cheer on their team.
Opposite below: Sadler shoots at goal.
Above inset: Busby stands with the trophy at Wembley.
Main picture: Twenty-two-year-old David Sadler on top of the world after helping United end their ten-year pursuit of the European Cup. It was from Sadler's cross that Bobby Charlton opened the scoring,

the ball glancing off the latter's balding pate early in the second half. Sadler played in 51 of United's 53 league and cup matches that season, switching from the half-back line to attack and back again with an ease befitting his versatile talents. Two years later, he was in Alf Ramsey's initial 28-man squad for the World Cup in Mexico, and got onto the pitch in the final warm-up match before the tournament started. Ramsey informed the Press who was

in his final 22, on the understanding that there would be a news embargo until he had spoken to the six unlucky players. One of the newshounds broke ranks and Sadler discovered he wasn't going to Mexico in a telephone call from his wife, who had been besieged by reporters asking for her reaction. Sadler won his fourth and final cap in November the same year, in a friendly against East Germany at Wembley.

# Ref's decision robs United of Cup double

Right: Matt Busby made European Cup success a personal crusade following the Munich tragedy. After three failed attempts, it all came right on 29 May 1968. Busby had turned an indebted club with a bombed-out ground into champions of Europe. Success was tinged with poignancy as the families of those who had died a decade earlier were invited to attend the victory celebrations.

Above inset: The victory celebrations begin. There was little smiling after 90 minutes at Wembley, when the score stood at 1–1. Busby berated his players for giving away possession too cheaply on a sultry night. Less than ten minutes later United had an unassailable 4–1 lead.

Top: Jubilant scenes as United show off the trophy to the fans after becoming the first English club to scoop Europe's top prize. The holders were warm favourites to retain the cup in 1968–69 but having disposed of Waterford, Anderlecht and Rapid Vienna, they faced AC Milan in the semis.

United went down 2–0 at the San Siro, finishing the game with 10 men after John Fitzpatrick was ordered off for kicking Milan's Swedish star Kurt Hamrin. It was a tall order to turn the tie round against one of the masters of the catenaccio defence, but United almost pulled it off. Charlton reduced the arrears, and with minutes to go United were robbed of the chance to take the game into extra time. After a goalmouth scramble the ball appeared to cross the line – confirmed by TV replays – but the referee waved away the claim. The momentum was with the home side and United would surely have gone on to win the tie had the referee not erred. The fact that Milan went on to thrash Ajax 4–1 in the final made the controversial incident all the more galling for Reds' fans.

# The glory boys

The 1967–68 United squad pose with the coveted European Cup. Although Matt Busby went into the transfer market more frequently to create his third great side, the team that took the field against Benfica was largely home grown. Only Alex Stepney, Tony Dunne and Pat Crerand joined for a fee – an aggregate investment of £116,000 – while seven members of the side came through the United ranks. The squad included a number of important bit-part players who contributed to the campaign. John Fitzpatrick (front row, right) found it hard to break the Stiles–Crerand half-back partnership and brought his terrier-like skills to bear at full-back in order to further his opportunities. By 1972, when the 26-year-old Scot would have found it easier to nail down a first-team place, he had developed an arthritic knee and left the game to become a wine merchant. Former Scottish schoolboys captain Francis Burns (middle row, second right) had displaced Shay Brennan for most of the season and was desperately unlucky to miss out on the Wembley final. Jimmy Rimmer (back row, third left) played only a handful of games in his 10 years at Old

Trafford. Busby made it clear that Stepney was his number one 'keeper, though he regarded Rimmer as too good to be allowed to leave the club. He got his long-awaited transfer under Tommy Docherty and enjoyed a late flourish to his career at Aston Villa, with whom he won the championship and the European Cup. Rimmer was an unused substitute against Benfica in 1968, and was forced to leave the pitch early in the Aston Villa–Bayern Munich final of 1982. The identity of the player who picked up two winners' medals in Europes's premier cup competition 14 years apart, having spent a total of less than 10 minutes on the pitch, made for a hardy perennial on the sports quiz circuit. The unluckiest man of all was Bobby Noble, who was in the middle of a long, painful and, ultimately, fruitless rehabilitation process when his team-mates were parading round the Wembley pitch with the European Cup. Noble, who captained the 1964 Youth Cup-winning side, had broken into the side in the title-winning season of 1966–67 but suffered horrific injuries in a car crash just as United were about to clinch the championship.

# 'Savagery'

Below: 25 September 1968. Shay Brennan, Bobby Charlton and Nobby Stiles on a shopping trip in Buenos Aires, the calm before the storm that awaited them in the first leg of the World Club Championship tie with Estudiantes. The omens weren't good. Feelings were still running high over the tempestuous England-Argentina World Cup match two years earlier, after which Alf Ramsey had branded the opposition 'animals'. The 1967 encounter between Celtic and Racing Club had been a better advert for fisticuffs than football. The United–Estudiantes games also saw a lot of blood spilt, the Manchester Evening News leading with the headline 'Savagery' after the 1–0 first-leg defeat. By the 1970s a number of European clubs – Liverpool among them – decided not to participate, threatening the future of the Europe-South America play-off. It was some time before the Club World Cup regained its prestigious place in the footballing calendar.

Right: Bobby Charlton pictured with daughters Suzanne and Andrea on a family holiday just after the European Cup victory of 1968. He had played in all but one of United's 53 games that season, scoring 18 times. Charlton's brace against Benfica in the Wembley final – one a rare header – were the only goals he scored in the nine-match European Cup campaign.

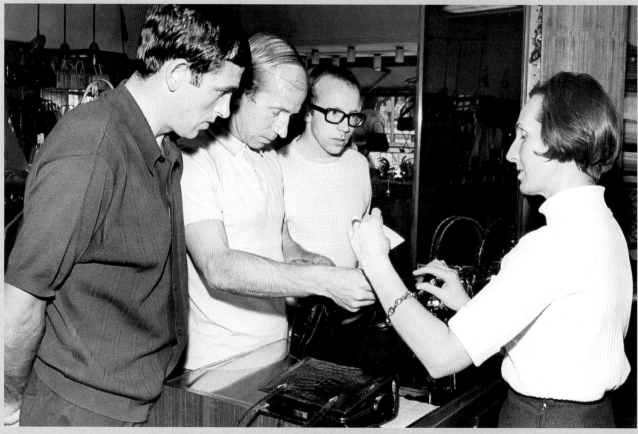

# 'Arise, Sir Matt'

Above and middle: Asked what he looked for in a player, Matt Busby said: 'Skill, fitness and character, and the most important of these is character.' The character of the United players was tested in the bruising two-legged encounter with Estudiantes in the 1968 Club World Cup. The matches were more like pitched battles than games of football. Stiles was dubbed 'The Assassin' by Argentine fans, and Estudiantes decided to get their retaliation in first, Nobby receiving a nasty facial wound after being head-butted. It wasn't merely the hard men who were targeted: Bobby Charlton needed stitches following an over-the-ball challenge. A string of X-rated challenges went unpunished and United players showed commendable restraint, although Stiles did eventually lose his cool, sent off for showing dissent to a linesman over an offside decision. United came away with a one-goal deficit and a queue for the treatment table. Matt Busby is pictured greeting greeting Estudiantes officials at Old Trafford before the return leg, and chatting to David Sadler, who was struggling with a leg injury. The second match followed much the same pattern as the first, the Argentine side responsible for some egregious foul play. Best and Hugo Medina were sent off for brawling, and the game ended 1–1 to give Estudiantes a pyrrhic victory. The crucial away goal was scored by Ramon Veron, whose son Juan Sebastian would join United for a then-club record £28 million in 2001.

Below left: A young autograph hunter tries to add a famous footballing moniker to his collection outside the team hotel after United's European Cup victory.

Below right: Matt Busby arrives at Buckingham Palace for the investiture ceremony that would confer a knighthood upon him.

# Decline and fall

Above: Bobby Charlton on the ball at Highbury, 26 December 1968, a game in which United went down 3–0 to Arsenal. Champions and runners-up in the previous two seasons, United slipped to 11th in 1968–69. There was a run to the quarter-final of the FA Cup, but it came courtesy of victories over Fourth Division Exeter City, Third Division Watford and Second Division Birmingham City – United needing a replay to get past the latter two opponents. Everton ended their interest with a 1–0 win at Old Trafford in the last eight. Why the great sixties team declined so rapidly has provoked much comment. Eighth in the league was the best United would manage in the next five years, with relegation lying at the end of the road. Ill luck played a part.

John Aston, the unlikely star of the Benfica match, suffered a broken leg in a local derby just three games into the new season. But, undoubtedly, removal of the foot from the gas pedal was also a factor. A collective sigh of relief was breathed as a heavy weight was lifted from the club's shoulders. It wasn't until the middle of the next decade that an exciting young team forged by Tommy Docherty began challenging for top honours once again.

Right: Bobby Charlton gets the better of Everton midfielder Colin Harvey on the opening day of the 1968–69 season. Charlton and Best scored in a 2–1 win at Old Trafford, but it wasn't a sign of what was to come. Nor was it a vintage season for Charlton, who weighed in with just five League goals.

# New man at the helm

Above: New boss Wilf McGuinness meets the squad as they report for pre-season training before the 1969–70 campaign. Initially, he was appointed first-team coach, though he was the de facto manager before that title was officially bestowed on him the following summer. Bobby Charlton was older than McGuinness, and the youngest Division One manager was undoubtedly hampered by the fact that he was a former teammate to some of the players. Inevitably, he lacked Busby's gravitas, but it was results that eventually counted against him. He took United to three semi-finals in little over a year at the helm, but in December 1970 the team stood 18th in the league, with just five wins in 23 games. After a League Cup exit at the hands of Third Division Aston Villa, the writing was on the wall for McGuinness. Villa winger Willie Anderson, who played in the 1964 Youth Cup-winning team alongside Sadler, Best and Aston, said of the 3–2 aggregate victory: 'On paper they should have killed us, but there seemed to be no heart in the club in those days.'
Middle right: Best gets up close and personal with Leeds' hard man Norman Hunter in a goalless draw at Old Trafford on 2 November 1968. Leeds went on to lift the championship, finishing 25 points ahead of mid-table United.

Below: Club rivalry is put aside as Sir Matt and Joe Mercer are invested as Barkers of the Variety Club of Great Britain in the summer of 1968. City's fall from grace was even more dramatic than United's. The champions finished 13th in 1968–9, though they did win the FA Cup, beating Everton – the side that put out United – en route to Wembley.

# Mr Consistency

**Far left inset:** Alex Stepney plucks the ball out of the air in a goalless draw at Upton Park, 29 March 1969.

**Main picture:** United's inconsistent form in the season following the European Cup win didn't apply to Stepney, who continued to make first-team action a rare occurrence for his talented understudy Jimmy Rimmer. Unfortunately for Stepney, England was blessed with considerable goalkeeping talent when he was in his prime, the likes of Banks, Shilton, Bonnetti and Clemence. In any other era he would surely have won more than his solitary cap, earned in a 3–1 win over Sweden a week before the Benfica match. It was a record his successors would have liked to emulate, 43 years would pass before another England 'keeper was on the winning side against the same opposition.

Singled out by Busby as the key to the 1966–67 title-winning campaign, Stepney was the only member of the team still around when United added the next piece of silverware to the trophy cabinet a decade later. The FA Cup victory over Liverpool in 1977 prevented the men from Anfield from winning the Treble, and thus rendered United's achievement 22 years later unique in the annals of English football.

**Above left:** George takes to the wheel of his Lotus Europa, an apposite mode of transport for one who lived life in the fast lane.

**Middle left:** January 1970. George is serenaded by singer Lucy Farrington, who had written and recorded a song dedicated to the United star. He had plenty of time on his hands to hear a rendition, for he was serving a four-week ban, following an incident in a League Cup semi-final defeat against Manchester City the previous month. Best had been in hot scoring form before the suspension, hitting 13 goals in 12 games. He was to celebrate his return to action with an even more remarkable goalscoring feat.

**Below left:** Prime Minister Harold Wilson presents Best with his award for finishing third in a Sportsman of the Year poll, behind Tony Jacklin and Lester Piggott. Wilson was Yorkshire born and served a Liverpool constituency, but he was a self-confessed Best fan.

# Rules of engagement

Best responds to his manager's exhortations to settle down by rushing headlong into an engagement with 21-year-old Danish beauty Eva Haraldsted, whom he had spotted among a crowd of autograph hunters during a pre-season tour that took in Copenhagen. Far from being pleased, Busby saw it as further evidence of his star's waywardness and irresponsibility. Needless to say, the liaison was short lived, though there was a sting in the tail as the wronged woman sued for breach of promise. The matter was settled out of court. There were plenty more beauty queens to come, though in his autobiography he refuted the charge that he had bedded seven Miss Worlds. 'It was only four,' George insisted. 'I didn't turn up for the other three.'

---

**Far from being pleased, Busby saw Best's becoming engaged as further evidence of his star's waywardness and irresponsibility.**

---

# The Theatre of Dreams

Right: Chairman John Henry Davies, the man who had saved United from going to the wall in 1902, had a vision for a ground befitting a team that had claimed its first League championship in 1908, and first FA Cup success a year later. He commissioned Archibald Leitch, the foremost stadium designer of his day, and Old Trafford opened for business 19 February 1910. Sandy Turnbull, one of the superstars of the era, carved his name in the record books as the scorer of the first ever goal, though United went down 4–3 to Liverpool. The

> No one has put it better than one of United's favourite sons, Sir Bobby Charlton, who called Old Trafford 'The Theatre of Dreams'.

ground in its original form may have had just one covered stand, but it represented a huge investment. The old Bank Street stadium had been sold off to the City Corporation for £5500; the new development cost around twelve times that figure. On the drawing board Old Trafford was conceived as a 100,000-capacity venue, but spiralling costs meant those ambitious plans had to be scaled back somewhat. The combination of a harsh economic climate and indifferent team meant few improvements were made before the Second World War, and a Luftwaffe raid in 1941 made Old Trafford an even sorrier sight. Since 1949, when the stadium re-opened its doors, there have been numerous development programmes, and on 31 March 2007 the latest of those saw a new Premiership attendance record set when 76,098 spectators watched United beat Blackburn 4–1. The capacity is now almost back to the 1910 figure of 80,000, though the numbers game tells but a small part of the story. Nor is it enough to describe Old Trafford as one of the pre-eminent sporting venues in the world, for that overlooks the cachet and rich history of a club that has a unique status within the game. No one has put it better than one of United's favourite sons, Sir Bobby Charlton, who called Old Trafford 'The Theatre of Dreams'.

Below left: It must have been gut-wrenching for Brian Kidd to sign off from United with the bitter taste of relegation in the mouth. Some 15 years later, he grabbed a second opportunity to help put United back on top, this time as part of the backroom team supporting Alex Ferguson. He worked his way through the ranks to become Ferguson's No. 2, having done sterling work bringing on the club's talented juniors. He had had a short spell as Preston boss in the mid-eighties and couldn't resist the lure of the top job at Blackburn when the call from Ewood Park came midway through the 1998–9 season. Six months later, Kidd was experiencing relegation as a manager, while United were basking in the glory of the magnificent Treble.

Below right: Brian Kidd shields the ball from 'Nijinsky' – Manchester City's England midfielder Colin Bell. United edged City in the League in 1969-70, though the blue half of Manchester had a rare double to celebrate in 1969–70. City also had the bragging rights with a League and Cup Winners' Cup double, a brief period of supremacy for the men from Maine Road.

# Busby moves upstairs

Above right: February 1969. Sir Matt considers the prospects for play with his old sparring partner Stan Cullis, who was now managing Birmingham City. A fixture pile-up did United no favours as they had to take on Blues in an FA Cup Fifth Round replay on 24 February, a mere 48 hours before the first leg of their European Cup quarter-final clash with Rapid Vienna. The Reds won both matches, which were vital to keeping the season alive as their championship hopes had all but disappeared by Christmas. Six months after being crowned European champions, United's results had dipped alarmingly. Of the 24 league fixtures played by the turn of the year, the team had won just seven. If not relegation form, it was bottom half of the table stuff. Busby had been unlucky in losing John Aston with a broken leg, but that loss was mitigated by the acquisition of Willie Morgan, who quickly became a terraces' favourite, something Aston never achieved. Unfortunately, some of the other new faces didn't fare quite so well. Carlo Sartori couldn't be mentioned in the same breath as the greats who had played up front, while it soon became clear that Steve James was no ready replacement for Bill Foulkes. Even though they were still in two cup competitions, Busby decided to call time. In January it was announced that he would relinquish responsibility for day-to-day team affairs and assume the position of general manager.

Below right: Matt Busby and Paddy Crerand on their way to the San Siro to face AC Milan in the European Cup semi-final. There was just one league match left when the Reds travelled to Italy for the first leg, with nothing riding on it. The entire season now rested on the Milan game. 20,000 packed into the Stretford End to watch the away leg on giant screens, a ground-breaking televisual move, though such fervent support thousands of miles from the action couldn't prevent United from sliding to a 2–0 defeat. At Old Trafford United could breach one of the meanest defences in Europe only once, though they were denied a second when claims that the ball had crossed the line after a goalmouth scramble were waved away by the referee. Television replays proved that the goal should have stood.

Above left: Highbury, 20 September 1969. Best on a jinking run that has two Arsenal defenders wondering whether to back off or dive in. Neither course of action was advisable. Best scored one and made another for Sadler in a game that ended 2–2.

Middle left: Best remained United's greatest asset and most consistent goalscorer at the start of the new decade.

Below left: The ever dependable Tony Dunne, rated by his manager as the best full-back in the world. Dunne won the Irish Footballer of the Year award in 1969 and was a regular first teamer until 1972–73, when he joined Bolton. His 530 appearances puts him seventh on the all-time list, behind Giggs, Charlton, Scholes, Foulkes, Gary Neville and Stepney.

**Right:** More fun and games off the field of play.

**Bottom left:** February 1970. A wave from George Best as he returns to action after a four-week ban, imposed for knocking the ball out of referee Jack Taylor's hands at the end of a League Cup semi-final against Manchester City in December. Francis Lee had won and scored a penalty five minutes from time, a crucial goal as it turned out, for the second leg at Old Trafford ended in a draw. Best's action was petulant rather than malicious, but the man who would go on to officiate at the 1974 World Cup final deemed it a misdemeanour worthy of the FA's attention. Best's comeback match was a Fifth Round FA Cup tie against Fourth Division side Northampton Town, who found him in irresistible form following his enforced lay-off.

**Bottom right:** Denis Law studies the runners and riders for the 1970–71 Division One race with sons Andrew and Robbie. Law would score 16 goals that term, a long way short of his best return. In his Manchester City days he equalled Best's feat of scoring six goals in a match.

# Crerand hangs up his boots

**Below right:** Paddy Crerand turned 32 during the 1970–71 season. Even though he was never a speed merchant, as a midfield player he was obviously coming towards the end of his career, and he called it a day at the end of this campaign, having played in around half of United's fixtures. It was often said that when Crerand played well, so did United. His exit, at a time when so many great players were in decline, was another problem for the in-tray of manager Frank O'Farrell in the 1971-72 season.

**Below left:** Many United fans would have sympathized with Best's frustrations about the side: too many ageing stars and too few quality players coming through the ranks or arriving via the chequebook, which contributed to his well documented flashes of indiscipline. Not long after Ian Ure's arrival from Arsenal for £80,000, one enterprising celebrity fan had the idea of collecting £2 from each of the 40,000 hard-core supporters to recoup the fee, upon which the Gunners could have had their shoddy goods returned to them. Wilf McGuinness later claimed that Ure's signing was imposed from above, by Sir Matt, an early indication of the difficulty he would face in trying to take United forward.

**Above:** The Lawman and Bestie tussle for the ball during pre-season training at The Cliff, July 1970. United would again finish eighth, 22 points adrift of champions Arsenal and just 20 ahead of bottom-placed Blackpool. A Third Round FA Cup exit at the hands of Division Two side Middlesbrough completed a mediocre season for the Red Devils. A run to the League Cup semi-final was the highlight of a turbulent 12-month period which saw Wilf McGuinness, Matt Busby and Frank O'Farrell all take the managerial reins. The fact that United were knocked out by Aston Villa, a Third Division side at the time, was yet another signal that United were entering a transition phase.

> When Crerand played well, so did United. His exit, at a time when so many great players were in decline, was another problem for the in-tray of incoming manager Frank O'Farrell.

# Cobblers hit for six

**Right:** 7 February 1970. Brian Kidd congratulates George Best on his stellar performance against Northampton Town in the 5th Round of the FA Cup. Best, fresh from his latest suspension, struck a double hat-trick that was top drawer, regardless of the calibre of the opposition. The Northampton full-back assigned to mark George that day described him as 'unplayable', while the overworked goalkeeper Kim Book – brother of Manchester City captain Tony – remarked: 'I don't think any of us knew where to look for him.' Northampton Town manager Dave Bowen bemoaned the fact that the FA hadn't banned him for five weeks instead of four. After disposing of Middlesbrough in the Sixth Round, United lost a titanic semi with Leeds, just a single Billy Bremner goal dividing the sides after three meetings. The FA introduced a third-place play-off for the FA Cup that season, which United won with a 2–0 win over Watford. It survived only one more season, but allowed United another first in the record books.

**Above:** Best shows his supreme control in the game where he hit Northampton for six. After Sir Matt moved upstairs to become general manager, Wilf McGuinness and Frank O'Farrell both struggled to bring George into line and prevent him from 'going missing' – with a host of beauty queens! Neither succeeded. Best was transfer-listed on 19 December, 1972, the day United dispensed with O'Farrell's services, and it later emerged that George had written to the club announcing his retirement from the game. Neither party carried the intention through, though the end of the Best era was fast approaching.

> **Best, fresh from his latest suspension, struck a double hat-trick. The Northampton full-back assigned to mark George that day described him as 'unplayable'.**

# Stein has change of heart

Top right: Newton Heath first met Woolwich Arsenal in a Division Two match on 13 October 1894. It was a 3–3 scoreline that day, Newton Heath going on to finish third in the league, the Gunners in mid-table. In the years since, the two teams have fought countless battles and enjoyed a special rivalry among English football's elite. Here, George Best leaves Arsenal skipper Frank McLintock and Eddie Kelly in his wake to set up a United attack.

revenge against the same opposition in the FA Cup Final. Chelsea had just thumped Watford in the semis to reach Wembley, while United had played out a 0–0 draw against Leeds. After a second goalless encounter, United went down 1–0.
Bottom: Best floored at White Hart Lane in 1970.

> **Wilf McGuinness was not first choice for the job. Jock Stein shook hands on a deal after a private meeting with Busby, but the Celtic boss subsequently had a change of heart, a decision he is said to have bitterly regretted.**

While the Reds spent most of the sixties challenging for honours and adding four major trophies to their cabinet, Arsenal were an average side.
Above left: Another brush with the law, but this time it's only a fan wanting Best's autograph.
Above right: Sport and pop stars have been regular visitors to Downing Street in the 'Cool Britannia' years. It happened less often in George's day, but, as was the case on the field, he was an exception.
Middle: Sir Matt Busby, in his new role as general manager, enjoys a joke with Nobby Stiles during United's trip to Stamford Bridge, 21 March 1970. Standing in the aisle is the man who was charged with following the biggest act in football. 31-year-old Wilf McGuinness was not first choice for the job. Jock Stein shook hands on a deal after a private meeting with Busby, but the Celtic boss subsequently had a change of heart, a decision he is said to have bitterly regretted. Whoever took over had a major rebuilding job on his hands. The side McGuinness fielded at Chelsea included Paul Edwards, Carlo Sartori and Ian Ure, while some stars of the golden era were on the wane. United went down 2–1, but were hoping to get their

# Luxury pad with absentee bachelor

**Below:** George Best's architect-designed bachelor pad in Bramhall was light years away from the homely comforts of Mrs Fullaway's lodgings in Chorlton-cum-Hardy. The luxuriously appointed 'Che Sera' came complete with snooker room, sunken bath and built-in 25-inch colour TV – and a hefty £35,000 price tag. To put that in perspective, his great mate Mike Summerbee thought he had splashed out when he paid £10,000 for his own Cheshire property, a large detached pile with stables in Hatherlow. United players weren't the best paid players in the league, for even when the maximum wage was abolished and Fulham proudly announced that they could now pay Johnny Haynes the £100 a week he was worth, Busby imposed a basic £35 maximum. He and Bill Shankly had an understanding regarding matters financial, the Liverpool boss taking exactly the same hard line to prevent a player haemorrhage up the East Lancs Road. However, George didn't have to rely on wages alone in order to afford a property worth far more than his manager's modest semi. He found there was easy money to be made through endorsements and advertising. A decade earlier, Duncan Edwards had been the face of Dextrosol glucose tablets, though his supplementary earnings were dwarfed by the fees Best accrued from deals that included advertising eggs in a high-profile television campaign and putting his name to a pair of football boots. In the two years that he owned the property George spent little time there, which meant that the fans camped outside were lucky if they caught a glimpse of their idol.

**Right:** On holiday in Spain in the summer of 1971 George plays the role of city gent when his company, George Best Boutiques, was floated on the Stock Exchange. At a stroke he made a paper profit of £3000.

# The Best family celebrate

Top: Beautiful blondes and equally head-turning motors were almost de rigueur for George. He got through a lot of models of each variety.

Above middle: George takes a rare trip home as parents Dick and Anne celebrate their silver wedding anniversary in 1970. Anne Best was teetotal until the age of 40, when she acquired a taste for alcohol that would contribute to her premature death in 1978. She was 54, five years younger than George was when a post-liver transplant infection claimed his life.

Below middle: Sir Matt Busby may have been exasperated and frustrated by some of George Best's antics but he never fell out of love with one of his favourite sons. 'We have had our problems with the wee fella, but I prefer to remember his genius.'

Bottom: George Best eats humble pie after his latest disappearing act. Days after arriving 90 minutes late for an FA Disciplinary Committee hearing and incurring a £250 fine for his trouble, Best failed to turn up for the trip to Stamford Bridge on 9 January 1971. Instead, he spent the weekend with actress Sinead Cusack. On his return to the side following a two-week suspension, Best finished the season strongly, scoring 12 goals in 17 games. A contrite Best said: 'I am satisfied I am playing for the greatest club in the world. The day I leave Manchester United will be the day they tell me they don't want me any more.'

'I am satisfied I am playing for the greatest club in the world. The day I leave Manchester United will be the day they tell me they don't want me any more.'

# Best sees red

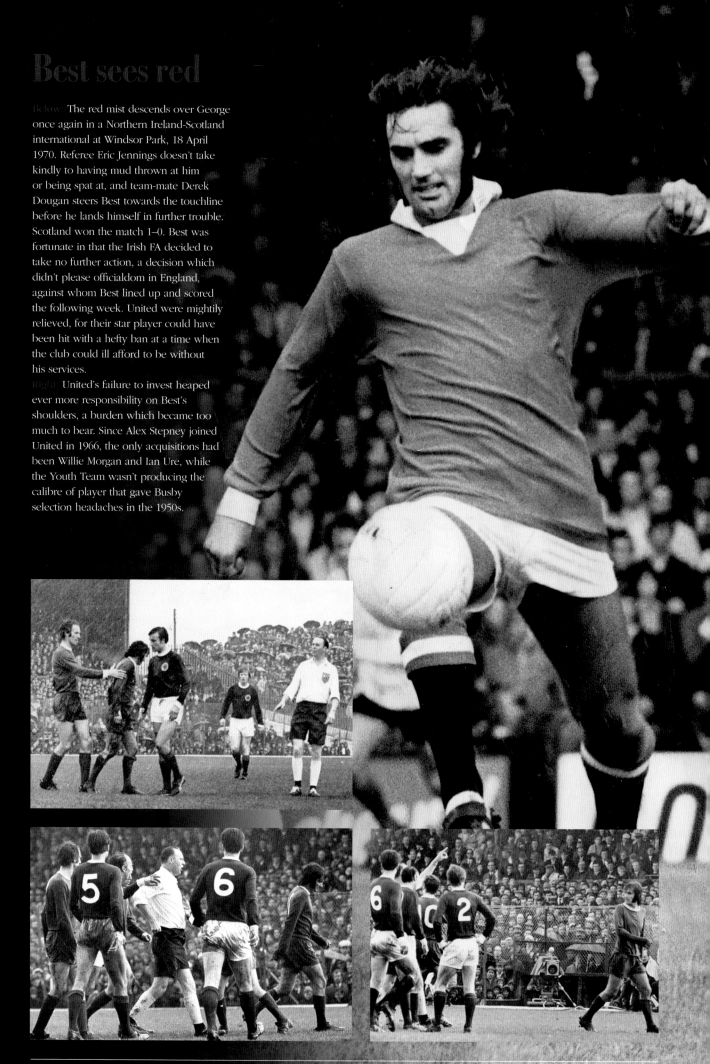

Below: The red mist descends over George once again in a Northern Ireland-Scotland international at Windsor Park, 18 April 1970. Referee Eric Jennings doesn't take kindly to having mud thrown at him or being spat at, and team-mate Derek Dougan steers Best towards the touchline before he lands himself in further trouble. Scotland won the match 1–0. Best was fortunate in that the Irish FA decided to take no further action, a decision which didn't please officialdom in England, against whom Best lined up and scored the following week. United were mightily relieved, for their star player could have been hit with a hefty ban at a time when the club could ill afford to be without his services.

Right: United's failure to invest heaped ever more responsibility on Best's shoulders, a burden which became too much to bear. Since Alex Stepney joined United in 1966, the only acquisitions had been Willie Morgan and Ian Ure, while the Youth Team wasn't producing the calibre of player that gave Busby selection headaches in the 1950s.

# O'Farrell takes a stand

**Above right:** When fair means for stopping Best didn't work, foul tactics were often attempted. After putting on a sparkling show in the first half of the 1971–72 season, George went AWOL once again. Unlike McGuinness, O'Farrell imposed a punishment and carried it through. Best was dropped, fined and made to do extra training. 'He is like a boy lost,' said the manager, whose hopes of helping Best find himself were to fall on stony ground. George's time was running out, though he did outlast O'Farrell on United's pay roll.

**Middle left and right:** Just two games into the 1971–72 season Best falls foul of the law yet again. Bobby Charlton shepherds him off the Stamford Bridge pitch and United coach Malcolm Musgrove makes sure there is no further incident on the touchline. Best went out of his way to get sent off – dismissed for remonstrating with referee Norman Burtenshaw over a booking handed out to team-mate Willie Morgan.

**Bottom right:** New boss Frank O'Farrell accompanies Best to a disciplinary hearing, which for once goes in the player's favour. The FA couldn't be sure that Best's abusive language was directed at Burtenshaw or – as Best insisted – at Morgan. The season started brightly for United, who took 32 points from their first 20 matches – including the incident-packed 3–2 win at Chelsea. Best was in sparkling form, banging in 14 goals in that period, and three more in the League Cup. It was to be the last time that the Old Trafford faithful would see George in his pomp, and it took United back to the top of the heap for the first time in three years. The table-topping form proved unsustainable. A wretched run of seven defeats on the spin in the new year saw the team slide down the league, while Stoke City were a thorn in United's flesh in both cup competitions. It showed that the malaise had been merely temporarily swept aside by the new managerial broom. United finished the season in eighth place, O'Farrell replicating McGuinness's achievement in the League and faring even worse in the cup competitions.

'As near perfection as a man and a player as it is possible to be'

After hanging up his boots, Paddy Crerand became part of the backroom team under Frank O'Farrell and Tommy Docherty, before striking out into management with Northampton Town.

Run-ins with referees were almost as commonplace as sublime finishes for Denis Law. Here he gets a finger-wagging from Roger Kirkpatrick in a 2–0 defeat for United at White Hart Lane, 4 March 1972. That made seven successive defeats in the League, which had the statisticians reaching for the record books. They found that United lost the opening 12 games of their 1930–31 programme, though that was of little comfort to Frank O'Farrell. A third successive eighth-place finish showed that this was a team in need of major surgery. Law's personal tally was just 13 goals in 41 league and cup appearances, and the fact that such a moderate haul was still good enough to make him the club's top marksman after Best told its own story.

'Among the great and happy things that have happened to me in my life has been the fact that I was Bobby Charlton's manager,' Sir Matt Busby once said. 'He was as near perfection as a man and a player as it is possible to be.' Charlton's respect and admiration for Sir Matt was just as great, a bond forged from triumph and tragedy. Busby had spent six months back at the helm when this picture (left) was taken, in June 1971. In the background are some of the latest crop of young hopefuls, including 16-year-old Sammy McIlroy. He was to be Busby's final signing, showing that the manager's eye for a young gem was as keen as ever.

George pictured in an all too familiar habitat in May 1971, having just completed a fourth successive season as United's top scorer. The drinking binges and disappearing acts continued for two-and-a-half more years, culminating in the final parting of the ways in January 1974. Best was frustrated at being the star of an average team, while his teammates resented his wayward behaviour. It was hardly conducive to a happy dressing room. Best's view on the subject: 'I was born with a great gift and sometimes that comes with a destructive streak.'

# The King 'dethroned'

*Top left:* Denis Law, 'the quickest thinking footballer I ever saw', according to Busby, bowed out at the end of the 1972–73 season, in unsavoury circumstances. After scoring 237 goals for United The King was given a free transfer by Tommy Docherty, who didn't bother to inform him that he was being evicted from his domain. Law decided he had one more year left in him, and jumped at the offer to rejoin Manchester City. His last touch of the ball as a professional came in a tense Old Trafford derby on 27 April 1974. His impish backheel won the game, though, contrary to the myth that subsequently took root, it didn't send United down. Other results meant Doc's team would have been relegated regardless.

*Top centre and middle, above right:* Limbering up for the 1972–3 season. Best had missed the pre-season tour of Denmark and Germany through suspension, his third club punishment in 18 months. On Frank O'Farrell's instructions he had moved in with the Crerand family in an effort to give his chaotic life greater stability. Paddy said he had high hopes for the new campaign, opining that George had played his best for less than half of the previous season, and still weighed in with 26 goals. It didn't quite work out as the recently retired midfielder hoped. Best scored just four goals in 19 league appearances, plus a brace against Second Division Oxford United in the League Cup. His time at Old Trafford was almost up, the final exit coming after a 3–0 defeat at Loftus Road on New Year's Day 1974. Those who pigeon-hole Best as a flawed genius, one who squandered his great gifts, should be reminded that he had ten years at the top and donned the United shirt 466 times. That was more appearances than, for example, Martin Buchan, who was with the club for a dozen years and considered a model professional. Best found the back of the net 178 times, putting him fifth in the all-time list. It wasn't until 1987–88 that another United forward hit 20-plus league goals in a season, though even Brian McClair might not place his achievement in the same bracket as Best's superlative showing 20 years earlier.

*Middle below right and bottom:* Best soaks up the sun in Majorca, one of his favourite holiday destinations. In the decade following the parting of the ways with United, he turned out for a string of clubs,

including Southern League Dunstable, a favour to team manager Barry Fry, who was a former Old Trafford clubmate. Not all his subsequent teams were made up of accountants and plumbers. At Fulham he lined up alongside Rodney Marsh, a partnership that produced flashes of the old magic. He also put on some marvellous exhibitions during his time playing across the Pond in the NASL. United fans prefer to remember him when he was at the height of his powers, the man who prompted Busby to remark: 'If ever there was a football genius, Best was that player. He had more ways of beating an opponent than any other player I have seen. The number of his gifts was unique and he made people gasp and laugh by his sheer audacity.'

In 1994 Bobby joined the exclusive ranks of the footballing knights, only the second player to be thus honoured, following Stanley Matthews into the record books.

# End of an era

Below left: Bobby Charlton in action in his 754th and final game for United, a 1–0 defeat at Stamford Bridge on the last day of the 1972–73 season and, above, still having fun training with Martin Buchan. Only Ryan Giggs has surpassed Charlton's appearance record, though the latter's 249-goal haul remains a club record. Charlton went on to manage Preston North End, for whom he also pulled on his boots, but with little success. Some put this down to the fact that his was a natural, instinctive talent and he lacked the analytical skills required of a manager. His personal qualities – essentially shy, self-effacing and tactful – probably didn't help. It was, perhaps, predictable that while the younger Charlton was an infinitely superior player, brother Jack would make a better fist of management. In 1994 Bobby joined the exclusive ranks of the footballing knights, only the second player to be thus honoured, following Stanley Matthews into the record books. Charlton remains a revered figure in the footballing fraternity, his very name evoking an abiding affection extending far beyond United's fan base. Right: Charlton and Best near the end of their careers.

# Busby spirit lives on

'Matt will seek the Board's advice, ponder over it, and then go away and do precisely what he wants to,' So said United chairman Harold Hardman of the man who shaped the club in the postwar period. Busby laid the groundwork for the success United has enjoyed in the last two decades, and, in particular, he laid down the blueprint for the style of football United fans have come to expect. He eschewed the win-at-all-costs mentality. Defeat was acceptable if you had given your all. The game was the most important thing. Sir Matt served the club for almost 50 years, taking on the role of President from March 1980 until his death on 20 January 1994 at the age of 84. Sir Matt was laid to rest in the club blazer and tie; it is scarcely surprising that his spirit still pervades the 'Theatre of Dreams'.

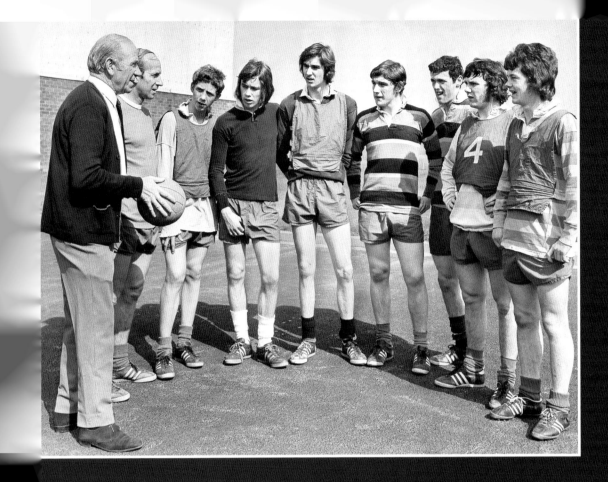

# Acknowledgements

The photographs in this book are from the archives of the Daily Mail.

Particular thanks to
Steve Torrington, Alan Pinnock,
Katie Lee, Dave Sheppard,
Brian Jackson, Richard Jones
and all the staff.

Thanks also to
Cliff Salter, Duncan Hill,
John Dunne and Wendy Toole